Esperanza

Esperanza
Edited & Compiled by Vishakha Naware
Paperback Edition

First published in India in 2023 by

Inkfeathers Publishing
Vivek Vihar, New Delhi 110095
www.inkfeathers.com

ISBN 978-93-90882-80-9

Esperanza

Hope is where the heart is!

Edited & Compiled by

Vishakha Naware

Inkfeathers Publishing

www.inkfeathers.com

DISCLAIMER

The anthology "Esperanza" is a collection of 14 short stories and 42 poems written by 29 authors who belong to different parts of the world.

Unless otherwise indicated, all the names, characters, objects, businesses, places, events, incidents—whether physical/non-physical, real/unreal, tangible/ intangible in whatsoever description used in this book are either the product of the author's imagination or used in a fictitious manner. Any resemblance to actual persons, objects, entities, living or dead, or actual events is purely coincidental.

The contents published in this book are solely owned by their respective authors and are in no way intended to hurt anyone's religious, political, spiritual, brand, personal or fanatic beliefs and/or faith, whatsoever. In case, any sort of plagiarism is detected in the contents within this anthology or in case of any complaints, grievances, or objections, neither the anthology editor nor the publisher is to be held responsible.

Featuring the writings of

Anannya Tiwary, Pushpa Bhatt, Revathi Bhasker,

Giridhar Uppala, Anju Elizabeth Kurien, Subhashree. S,

Karan Bhanot, Shivali Singh, Mallika Chandrasekhar, Adwaith Jayan,

Smruti Tilak, Carol Mitra, Kavita Singh, Anushka Rathi, Srishti Sareen,

Dinaz Treger-Patel, Sanika Sajan, Sumakalyani Ganti, RaShiMa Roy,

Kirti Pradeep, Gayatri Bhasker, Malika Mehta, Dimple Makkhija,

Tanushree Keshan, Deepika Chalke, Supraja Raghuram,

Gairik Misra, Avinash Sadaphule, Vishakha Naware

CONTENTS

MEET THE EDITOR

Vishakha Naware is a foreign language trainer, content and fiction writer, and poet. Languages are not only her bread and butter, but also her passion. A former journalist by profession, she loves weaving stories and telling tales. She is also a keen observer and likes to use her observations in her writing. She is also an inquisitive traveller and a culture enthusiast and loves to explore and learn about new places and people. She loves to cook and bake, read fiction books and, binge-watch thrillers in her leisure time.

ACKNOWLEDGEMENTS

It is indeed surreal to see my name on the front cover of a book! I have many people to thank for this achievement. Starting with my parents, parents-in-law, my brother and my close friends who motivated me to challenge my boundaries and start writing regularly.

I would like to thank the Inkfeathers Team for giving me this opportunity. I extend my gratitude towards the publishing manager, Uma Bokil, who answered all my queries and guided me throughout this process.

I am highly indebted to all my co-authors, who believed in me, supported me and were very patient during the process of publishing this book.

Last but definitely not least, I would like to thank my supportive husband, Pushkar and my wonderful son, Vihaan. They both motivate me to strive for better in life!

EDITOR'S NOTE

Fiction writing has been my passion since childhood, but I could give it wings only during the pandemic times. I first saw my name in a book in December 2020 and it felt surreal to see my thoughts materialised on paper!

Many a time, writing is cathartic and through words and paragraphs we can put our feelings on paper, sometimes those feelings which we couldn't share with anyone. Writing gave me a medium to channelise my overwhelming emotions and create poetry and write stories related to everyday life.

Editing this anthology has been a dream come true. The theme "Esperanza" or "hope" has been very close to my heart. Life is unpredictable and we all endure heartbreaks, sometimes toxic relationships and other difficulties which leave us wounded and scarred.

Hope is something that motivates you to not only survive but also thrive through the ups and downs of this journey called life. This motivation and inspiration make us rise like a Phoenix through ashes and we come out stronger and more resilient.

The stories in this book will serve as an inspiration to minds that have endured hardships in life: be it in a relationship, friendship or within the family or at the workplace. These stories written by writers belonging to different age groups and from all over India, Australia and the United States, aim to brighten up your spirit and serve as a much-needed warm and cosy hug after a heartbreak!

I wish you enjoy the stories and poems written by 29 authors, who have put their heart and soul into this book! Happy Reading!

An Ode to Hope

Vishakha Naware

Act of true courage of a brave soul,

It's just hope that helps you achieve your goal.

Open your eyes and breathe in now,

To the unfailing faith, you bow.

Say aye to pure spirit!

When everything seems black, jaded,

Memories torn; faces faded.

When all but in ether, you float,

There is no happiness to note.

Say aye to the brave spirit!

When loneliness and sorrow surround,

Anger and indifference hound.

Believe in pure love and kindness,

All the world needs is gentleness.

Say aye to the free spirit!

In ever-evolving wisdom,

Lies unwavering optimism.

Hope is in the way that you smile,

How would you go that extra mile?

Say aye to true spirit!

An Encompassing Embrace

Kavita Singh

When a storm wreaks havoc in life,
And leaves emotions mortal on the floor,
It pains terribly to bend and pick them up,
As it is heavy to endure the heart sore.

When life takes much more than,
What you have got and earned,
It seems all in vain in a blink and,
What you nourished so long is burned.

To evoke life in your dead soul,
Something comes out of the blue,
To soothe your aching heart, and
To assemble scattered bits of you.

Autumn comes to take away yellows,
And leaves your heart alone and dry.
Spring is waiting there to make you,
Green, shiny, and light to fly.

No matter how dark is your room,
To enlighten it, rays of hope find their way.
To see life from a new perspective,
Every night is followed by a bright day.

The heavens are covered over the Earth,
In an encompassing embrace.
To not leave your heart broken for long,
Change is constant, by Almighty's grace.

Levántate (Wake Up)

Anannya Tiwary

The winds you felt,

The storms inside you that dealt,

They walked past you many times,

And you thought you felt more alive.

Fragile peonies that bloomed inside of you,

Were disguised nightshades with sharp blades.

All that is now a memory,

It now feels so gloomy.

It's been months and years,

Still, their remembrance makes you stir,

It's like you are paralysed,

But it isn't too late to realise.

That it's not the end, honey,

Someone better is waiting patiently,

So, you have got to get up from the ruins,

Heal those bruises!

It wasn't love, was it?

Just a tingly feeling of a past gone beloved,

In some days, weeks, and months,

Their memory won't hurt as it did once.

In fragrant white clouds,

You'll wander and be found.

Be a whole new person,

Remember to live and learn.

Wings of Hope

RaShiMa Roy

The thundering applause was deafening. As Noyonika walked up the stage to receive the Filmfare award for the best actress, her eyes welled up with tears. It was almost surreal. The glitz and glamour of the Mumbai film industry were enough to blind anyone, but what this simple girl from Saharanpur experienced at this moment was a heady mix of emotions. All at once, she was enthralled, proud, elated, and grateful, but there was a tinge of melancholy that had never left her. Not since the night she had mustered up the courage to run away from home.

Home—how she had longed to have one of her own. A space she could call her own, one that she could decorate the way she wanted to, one in which she would spend happy moments with her husband and children. Her friends would often tease her about not having any ambition in life. Of course, she had an ambition: to be a good homemaker, a loving wife, and a doting mother. 'Was there anything wrong with that?' she often thought. Not according to her mother though, who often told her that her good looks would make sure she got married into a wealthy family.

Noyonika hoped her life would be more comfortable than it was at her parents' place. Her father's job as a university professor ensured they were considered a respectable family. Nevertheless, their standard of living remained very simple. And then when Noyonika turned 23, as anticipated by her mother, they received a marriage proposal from Kanpur. Noyonika's dreams had come true. With Shridhar, it was love at first sight for her. He was the son of a wealthy businessman from Kanpur—tall, handsome, well-spoken, and gentle. It seemed like a match made in heaven. Shridhar's parents and sister did seem a bit intimidating, but Noyonika and her parents accepted that as one of the several compromises that one has to make in life. It was a small price to pay for the wonderful life she would be leading. Or so they thought.

The first few months of her marriage were indeed a breezy romance, straight out of the films, that Noyonika had grown up watching. Shridhar pampered her to the hilt with weekend getaways, expensive gifts, and his adorable loving ways. She in turn was the perfect partner, cooking his favourite dishes and looking after his every need. Life couldn't have been better for Noyonika. But the occasional sarcastic comments of her mother-in-law could be piercing. Noyonika hated conflicts and avoided any confrontations. However, the unnecessary reprimanding increased with every passing day. Her mother-in-law and sister-in-law would make fun of her choice of clothes, criticise her cooking, and leave no stone unturned to make her feel inferior. Gradually, the difference in the social standards of her parents' family and her husband's family was glaring at her like an ugly reality. After having managed to avoid telling Shridhar anything for eight months, Noyonika broke down one night in front of him. What perplexed her was his reaction.

He heard her out patiently. And then as though nothing had happened, he began to talk about their upcoming plans for the weekend. Noyonika was confused. Could Shridhar simply not fathom what she had been going through? The next time she narrated an incident to him, he thought she was overreacting. On yet another occasion he promised that he would speak to his mother. A promise that he did not keep.

Over time, Noyonika realised that Shridhar was just not capable of taking a stand for her. When she spoke to her mother about her difficult situation, her mother advised her to have a child. 'The child will solve all problems and bring abundant happiness,' said her mother. Noyonika certainly did not want to have a child out of a relationship which was not complete in itself. She then confided in Shridhar's aunt, who explained his point of view to her. Shridhar had grown up with the belief that friction between the wife and the mother was bound to happen. It is, therefore, best to not get involved and let things resolve on their own. Sadly, all of life's complications do not resolve on their own.

Noyonika tried hard to please her mother-in-law and to connect with her sister-in-law. Unfortunately, nothing worked. She felt increasingly depressed and began questioning her self-worth. This is not the life that she had wanted to live. She was tired of putting up this charade of a happy daughter-in-law. Moving out of the family home into a nuclear family setup was an unacceptable thought in her conservative family.

Her dream of a perfect marriage was fading right in front of her eyes. She felt helpless and dejected. It was as though her life was spiralling out of control. Her state of mind was beginning to reflect in her physical appearance as well. The dark circles were apparent, and this version of Noyonika was a far cry from her cheerful and loving self. She began to hate herself and started to doubt her self-respect. Her relationship with Shridhar had to bear the burden of her sadness too. There was an unsaid distance that was gnawing at their relationship. Even his love and fondness for her were not enough to keep this marriage going. Noyonika knew that she had to make a choice. It was a choice between her self-respect and her love for her husband, who refused to speak up for her.

Not able to bear the burden of living a superficial life, she decided to walk out of the marriage. Going back to her parents' home was not an option. Her parents would face a lot of flak from society because of her and she did not want to hurt them. One night she found herself at Kanpur station boarding a train to Mumbai. An old school friend, Mithali was settled in Mumbai. Noyonika had contacted her, and Mithali had agreed to put her up till her husband, a sailor, would return from his four-month sojourn on the ship. Noyonika had four months to make something out of her life. And she had no clue how she would do that.

Given her stunning looks, Mithali suggested that Noyonika try her hand at modelling. Noyonika sold some of her jewellery to put together a portfolio. Then started the endless rounds of the agencies, producers, and any contact that was forwarded to her. The tiring travelling in Mumbai and rude rejections did dampen her spirit at times. To add to that was the pressure of her dwindling finances and the fact that she had limited time to get a break.

Nevertheless, Noyonika battled on and did not give up hope. Finally, it happened. She got her first break with a print campaign for a saree brand. She cried with her head in Mithali's lap when she got her first payment. Now there was no looking back. Noyonika was picked up by several agencies for their ad campaigns and soon was also selected for ramp modelling. It was not an easy journey to become a part of the Mumbai Brigade, which was not welcoming to outsiders from small towns. But by now, Noyonika knew how to conduct herself at the parties. She had rented a small apartment in Bandra, a leafy suburb of Mumbai. She had come a long way from the small-town girl of Saharanpur and the subdued daughter-in-law of the Kanpur family. Little did she know what was in store for her.

On one of her ad film shoots she was spotted by a film director, who was looking for a fresh face. She was asked to audition and got selected for the role. Though she was awkward in her first film, Noyonika got offers from other big banners. Her strong screen presence could not be ignored. Soon she bought her apartment, had her car, and even started supporting her parents financially. Who would have thought that the girl with no ambitions whatsoever would one day rule Bollywood? She wondered if Shridhar ever remarried. She wasn't sure if the aching feeling in her heart was a longing for Shridhar, or simply for a life partner. Of course, a lot of men had shown interest in Noyonika, but nobody had truly captured her heart, the way Shridhar had.

Tonight, at the after-awards party organised by Filmfare she was the centre of attention. The A-listers of the industry were all there celebrating her success with her. Despite all the adulation, that feeling of sadness refused to leave her.

She was staring at her glass of wine when a man came up to her and introduced himself as the new editor of a well-known magazine. His eyes and gaze took her breath away. There was a warmth in his eyes that she had not felt in a long time. As the evening progressed, they were increasingly attracted to each other. He gently took her hand in his and said, 'Noyonika, I want to get to know the real you.' She smiled coyly and he added, 'Would you tell me your real name, to begin with?' She stared at him for a few seconds and then answered shyly, 'My name is Aastha, and you know what Aastha means?'

'It means *hope*.'

Finding Myself

Carol Mitra

I feel so stuck in this bottomless pit,

I don't know how I got here,

I don't know where I'd go,

All I can see at the very top,

A glimpse of sunlight penetrating,

Through a tiny hole.

I've tried many times to crawl,

Back towards the light,

The shame was woven into me,

I hid in its shadow and lay down below,

The walls are so slippery,

There's nothing to hold on to!

Am I the only one who's ashamed?

Even though it's your eyes I look into,

I cry, I scream, I rage. I feel I'm expressing myself.

But I'm drowning inside my head,

I count the days, one mark at a time,

On the wall, till I can clearly see ten,

My fingers hold on, they match my weary hands,

I hold on gently, and then a firm grip,

As I find my confidence!

If I have learnt to grow from pain,

If I still have a breath and a belief,

Then certainly you can. Come!

I can walk you through my story!

The Black and Red Butterfly

Gayatri Bhasker

Sitting this morning with my sister and mother,
Yet my heart is constantly thinking of my father.

We are looking at the beautiful flowers and butterflies,
Seeing the tiny birds and hearing the cuckoo's cries.

Sunshine makes everything look clear and bright,
But I feel blank, and nothing seems right.

My heart feels empty, incapable of love,
Missing my dad who's gone far up above.

Why did he have to leave all of a sudden?
Maybe he got tired of all of his burdens?

Both God and him; they fooled us all the way,
Giving some hope and then snatching it away.

I think of many things to feel pacified,
But each thought seems shallow; I'm not satisfied.

All we have left of him are memories,
Some of his things and a few stories.

I can feel his shoulder, as I rested my baby head,
When he used to carry me; to put me to bed.

I can feel his pat on my back,
His reminders when I used to slack.

He was reassuring; always there for me,
Ever cheering and encouraging me.

He used to wave at me till the end,
And I waved back too as the train went over the bend.

All I have left now are these fleeting visions,
It's so hard to be practical and accept the situation.

Just now I had started to relate to him,
In different roles—as a parent or spouse.
How to handle situations, in or out of the house.

How do I ask my unspoken questions now,
Can I get one more chance, will God allow it?
How do I discover the man of 71 years?
Time spent in struggles, hard work and fears.

Despite this, he was full of cheer,
Only these facts are now my souvenirs.

The chasing squirrels bring me back from my reverie,
Looks like they have made a discovery.

As we sit watching life go by,
In comes a huge black and red butterfly!

It comes so close to us and flutters,
Goes to my mom, then sister and I muttered,

Is that Appa? Has he come in this form?
Is it a message from him? Is that the new norm?

It flies off just as fast as it had come,
We all break into smiles, far from being glum.

Appa has sent us a magical sign,
He's with us, despite being one with the Divine!

Yes, I should lead my life with this belief,
Sensing him in any form brings such relief.

Sunshine makes everything look clear and bright,
Suddenly my heart feels so light.

I realise he lives on everywhere and even in me,
He is the root, and I am now the tree!

Breath of Life

Sanika Sajan

The same fire burning me inside out,
Shattered deeply from within.
Still, they tell me to let off,
Like my heart was just a lump of ice,
To melt in those emotionless words,
My life was never mine.
Every choice was made for someone,
Now, I think it's time to put a stop,
Walking out and breathing back freely.

Freely to the time, I smiled more,
Days I cared for my happiness.
A small crowd of encouraging peers,
Wanting to live more on those days.
The only hope for a new start,
And a better life with smiles,
No regrets, no worries!
Enjoying every step I take,
In the process of building,
A new version of myself.

What Next?

Revathi Bhasker

Hansini looked around her. She was frightened, to say the least. She found herself in some sort of a forsaken warehouse, tied to a chair with strong ropes. She tried to shout and scream for help but felt stifled as her mouth was plastered. Barrels and cartons were surrounding her and the door in front seemed to be latched from the outside.

She had married Khushal just a week before and both of them had just arrived at Kodaikanal in Tamil Nadu for their honeymoon. They were relaxing by the side of the lake when Khushal received a call. The expression on his face changed and he immediately told Hansini that he had to attend to some urgent and unavoidable work. He escorted her to the resort where they were staying and left in a hurry. He asked her to keep the door open as he would be back very soon.

At this moment, she was bound to the chair and her thoughts were racing back to the past. Hansini had lost her parents in a fire accident in a factory where they worked. Being their only offspring, Hansini was entitled to insurance and compensation, but as she was a minor, her uncle collected the money on her behalf as her guardian. Little did she realise that her uncle was waiting for the day she turned eighteen when he planned to get everything transferred to his name!

She recalled that it was her birthday—she was turning eighteen. Her uncle, Purushottam, had planned an elaborate celebration. The decorations were of the highest class, and it looked as if it was a fairyland. As the band played the birthday song, she was cutting the huge cake when there was a power outage. There was a commotion and while some switched on the torches in their mobiles, others were just screaming and pushing each other. Hansini was tossed here and there and suddenly found herself in the arms of a stranger. She felt secure and the pleasant musk perfume drew her closer to him. She was floored. When the lights came on, she saw him clearly and said to herself that THIS was her man. He too seemed to reciprocate the same feelings and would not let go of her.

Soon normalcy was restored and the party which had got disrupted for a few moments was in full swing. Purushottam comforted Hansini and introduced him to Khushal. The very next day, her uncle invited Khushal for lunch and to Hansini's pleasant surprise, their wedding was fixed. Hansini was on cloud nine and now started counting the days until the happy occasion.

Purushottam hosted a grand wedding and a happy Hansini set off with Khushal with sweet dreams of a happy life. They first went to Khushal's house from where he collected his clothes and other things before setting off to Kodaikanal for their honeymoon. Hansini was speechless on seeing the grandeur of her new home and could not believe her luck in finding such a fine match.

In the resort where he had left her, Hansini was looking at wedding photographs and trying to remember relationships, when she heard someone at the door. It was not *someone* but many men. There were at least four of them and all looked like ruffians, for that was what they were. Before she could understand what was happening, one of them cupped her face and she fainted instantly.

When she recovered, she understood that everything was amiss. At that moment the phone rang. The ruffian picked it up and put it on the speaker for others to hear the instructions and act accordingly.

They were all in the adjacent room, but the voice rang loud and clear. To Hansini's horror, it was her husband, Khushal's voice!

'*Kya kar rahi hai woh* (What is she doing)?' he barked. Gone was the softness in his voice. It was totally brutal and business-like. He ordered them to take utmost care of her and see that she does not run away. He said that she would be 'sold' that night for Rs. 50 lacs. He also told them that when Purushottam came to collect his commission, he should be told that Khushal was away and could not be reached.

Hansini's heart skipped a beat. She could not believe that Uncle Purushottam too had a role to play. Suddenly, she heard his voice. 'Where is Khushal?', he roared. 'I have so many bills to settle, and he is trying to run away from me without paying my commission of Rs. 20 lacs. Even that is a small sum for a beautiful talented virgin. I should have negotiated myself without his mediation.'

He looked around for Khushal but did not find him, so he left in a huff. As Hansini had been bound in a dark corner, he did not see her for otherwise he would have taken her away till such time he got his money!

In a few moments, the gang came up to her. One of them held out a foil pack and asked her to eat out of it. He freed her hands and removed the tape on her mouth but before that, he securely fastened her to the chair by tying her body and feet. Hansini was both disillusioned and disgusted. Both the men in her life—one who raised her and the other who was just married to her—were only interested in making money out of her!

The men left her with the foil pack and a bottle of water. Hansini looked around to see if she could find anything that could cut the rope and give her a chance to escape, but she could not find any such thing. Soon the henchmen started talking in the next room. Khushal was to come only that night to hand over Hansini. They were all quite hungry and yearned for some rum too. One was sent to get the food and drink while the others kept watch.

He had to cross the room where Hansini was kept in bondage. While whistling his way, he put his hand into his pocket to take out the money and count it. Unknown to him, the penknife in his pocket, too, came out and, as luck would have it, landed on Hansini's dress. Once he was gone, with her freed hands, Hansini cut off the ropes that tied her and quietly moved to the next room and bolted the door from outside, locking up the other gangsters in that room. She then got out of the building.

She drew the *dupatta* over her head to conceal her face and walked stealthily and swiftly. She did not wish to be caught by those men again. While walking on the curb, she spotted Khushal's car halt at the signals. In fright, she rushed into the first house she could see and knocked at the door.

A middle-aged woman opened the door and took her inside. One look at the interiors made Hansini realise she had probably jumped from the frying pan to the fire. The lady, Kashibai, was only too happy to see her and lost no time to fix up a date for her the very same evening. Hansini trembled but now had nowhere to go. She was trapped, or so she felt. Just then, Munna entered. Seeing him, Kashibai was relieved. 'I was waiting for you. I just have to go to the bank and come. Until such time you can take care of the house. I am delighted to share that we have a prize catch this afternoon, which walked into our house!' she exclaimed.

Munna turned around to see Hansini in a corner. One look at her, and he felt some bonding between them. As soon as Kashibai left, Hansini mustered courage and called out, '*Bhaiya*!' Munna extended his hand. 'Don't worry, *behna* (sister)! I will see what I can do for you.' He listened to her story, and tears rolled down his cheeks when she finished. He hugged a confused Hansini and comforted her, 'I recollect the match factory very well. You may not know, but I was the firstborn to our parents, and when our father saw that I was not normal, he simply gave me away to an *ayah* in the hospital and told our mother that the child was stillborn. When I was old enough to understand, the *ayah* took me to the factory and showed me, my parents. You were just born, and they were cuddling you when I saw them. At first, I was envious, but soon after when I came to know of the fire in which our parents had perished, I came to the site with the ayah to try and bring you with me, but our uncle preceded me, and I did not know where he took you. It is destiny that has brought us together. Have hope. Something good will come to us,' he said.

Hansini felt tremendously happy and safe. Soon, Kashibai returned and after lunch, she went to her room to rest. Munna immediately came down and quickly asked Hansini to follow him discreetly. Munna had with him his earnings and with that, they first bought themselves tickets for the very first train that would be departing to a far-off destination. Munna knew that it would not be long before Kashibai started her search for them, but he was sure that she would never imagine that they would have made their escape by train.

The next evening, they found themselves in Kolkata. Munna had his way of getting things done within a few days. They had set up a fast-food stall outside Victoria Memorial. He managed to find themselves a single-room tenement where they settled down comfortably.

Within a few days, the stall picked up very well and they were earning profits. At the back of her mind, Hansini harboured fears of Purushottam, Khushal, and Kashibai and would quite frequently get up in the middle of the night with a bad dream, but Munna's comforting hand was always over her shoulder.

One evening as they were busy attending to customers, a car drew to a stop a few stalls away from theirs and a couple got down. The woman pointed out to Munna's stall and insisted that they should eat there. Hansini caught sight of Khushal from the corner of her eye and signalled to Munna and went and hid.

Hansini had alerted the fellow stall owners that the man accompanying the woman was the one who wished to trade her to a wealthy man. The unity among the group was unprecedented. Khushal followed the lady albeit hesitantly, as he was not used to eating on footpaths. When she neared Munna's stall and asked to be served her favourite dishes, Munna's friends circled Khushal and dealt blows to him. When the lady protested, Munna asked her, '*Inka naam Khushal hai kya?* (Is his name Khushal?)' When she said that it was true, he then alerted her that she would meet the same fate as his sister and that it was better that she stayed away from him.

The lady was shocked and couldn't believe what she heard but when Hansini came out of her hiding and told her story, she was convinced. She immediately made a phone call and within minutes, police arrived at the scene. The lady's father was the Deputy Commissioner of Police, and it was not long before Khushal was taken into custody.

Hansini felt relieved and thanked the lady. She too was happy that she was saved from a trap and wished to help Munna and Hansini. She arranged to find a small shop on rent in the heart of the city and got them to start their business there. Needless to say, the small eatery flourished and in a very short time, it became a restaurant. By the end of the year, on Christmas, it was reopened as *Esperanza*, an elite hotel which found its place in google maps too and attracted many a footfall.

Move On!

Smruti Tilak

Promises made, hope in the air,

Honest talks, oh what a flair!

Each act so rare,

Genuine was your care.

Picture perfect, brilliant collage,

Reality struck, like a mirage.

Dreams crippled,

Agony tripled.

Volcano of emotions, erupted lava molten,

Shattering tears soaked the drapes of my cotton.

Different paths, destiny had chalked,

Never again, together we walked.

All alone I was in this deep dark night,

It was my battle that I had to fight.

Even the darkest night has to end,

When the radiant rays at dawn shine with brilliance.

Forget the bygones, ignore the scars,

Vanquish your dark past like the celestial yellow star.

Not every relation is blessed with love and compassion,

If there is no mutual respect, it is wise to end the association.

Live for those who love you,

Let go of those who walked away from you.

Create your own path with confidence,

Value your identity and your existence.

It's never late to make a new beginning,

Pure bliss is to surrender to the Supreme being.

Destiny had better plans, move on with grace,

Hope is a waking dream, accept and embrace it.

Little Things

Kavita Singh

Hope comes from the hole,

Through which we never try to peep.

It shows those vivid things,

Which may help us to leap.

Sometimes thoughts turn our paths,

Cumbersome to travel,

But small things change the way and

Pave our roads as gravel.

Nature has given power,

For everyone to look forward.

When it comes to breathing,

Trees even grow, their roots upward.

We learn and evolve with skills and
Some we possess from eternity.
Things with strong belief reach,
Their destination with serenity.

We must live each and every day,
Of life as a beginner with a zest.
Little things are always waiting,
To make us prepared for the next.

Wanderer

Anju Elizabeth Kurien

I wanted to run as far as ever could,

Nothing reminded me of my belongingness.

I stripped all those dark barks,

I shed all those dead leaves.

I let loose my waves on those sharp thorns,

My toes touched the lush green fresh.

But failed to soothe the ruth,

And never lulled them to deep sleep.

Those lilies were ghast trophies of the slain,

As approached the furthest,

I saw the darker and lighter shades of green,

Whose flawless darling azure caressed the buds to bloom.

I saw there a filter of twigs for the rays,

As I filtered my silhouette, I cleared the way,

The forest's bundle twisted the mystery,

I found my palace of solitude to be savoured in solace.

The castle, the grave and its wilderness,

where its wrecks like those petals bloomed,

aspired to shower my palette in those colours,

I left the shadows of my past there.

Like a serpent, I shed my reality,

Took refuge in those fluffy fur beds,

In the company of the huge world of those tiny,

I hugged back nature to be nurtured further.

Who shook me off the beautiful world?

I woke up only to be shattered,

Back to the world, they said,

They say this to be real.

For me, they are nothing but fools,

Who defeated me of my expectations,

Who forced me out of my asylum,

Who let me out to be so vulnerable.

I didn't want it to be my childhood fantasy,

If so, I would have loved to remain there,

As no illusions of this cage are jovial,

I would better be a wanderer forever!

Grandma's Love

Kirti Pradeep

Grandma heard Amit giggling in the adjacent room, as he watched a cartoon on the television. The sound of his happy and relaxed laughter filled her with a warm feeling of contentment and brought a smile to her lips.

'I am glad my child has learnt to enjoy his childhood again,' she said. She kept the newspaper aside as she remembered that day two weeks ago when a frail and unsure-looking Amit had stood in her doorway with his mother.

The first thoughts that had crossed her mind when she had seen her 12-year-old grandchild were, 'Why is he looking so unhappy and forlorn? Will I be able to take care of him? Will he like to stay with me in this small town?'

Grandma knew that she was the last hope for Amit's mother, Suman. She was going to meet Suman, her daughter-in-law, after a long gap of 8 years. And so, was well aware that the child had no choice whatsoever. 'Is the thought of living with me making Amit so sad?' she wondered as she saw him. She had lost touch with them so many years back!

She often wondered what had gone wrong between her son and

Suman. After all, they had been friends and classmates at the University for a few years. She had gladly accepted Uday's choice, and being his only living parent, she, with the help of a few close relatives, had arranged their marriage. She had liked Suman during their short stay together before the couple had left for Australia to pursue their dream jobs. Their visits once every few years thereafter had been too short to get acquainted, and then, with Amit's arrival, every visit had revolved around his activities alone. She couldn't get enough of his company during the visits.

And then, one day, she got a call from Uday, 'Ma, Suman and Amit are returning to India permanently.' She had been very hopeful that they would come to meet her. But that hope had died gradually as months passed into years with no information about them. Whenever she had tried to broach the topic with Uday during his visits, his stilted responses had discouraged her from being too inquisitive. She had given up in the past few years though she had often prayed for the wellbeing of her grandchild. And she felt overwhelmed to see him again in front of her. She hugged him tightly, but he didn't remember her at all now. His sad looks seemed to make him doubt whether he would like the old lady standing in front of him.

He had been polite but aloof the next day. Every time he spoke to his mother, his eyes seemed to question her. He seemed to ask her, 'How can you leave me alone here and go on your office tour? What if Grandma is as uncaring and disinterested as the other caretakers and maids had been? How can I manage alone with her in this new place?'

Grandma remembered how he had gradually opened up in the coming days after Suman had left. They both had thoroughly enjoyed their outings, story reading sessions, playing cards and even chatting with each other. Amit had been very interested in his Papa's childhood photos and all the tales of his childhood. And he had been full of questions recently, such as 'When does Papa come to India? Does he talk about me? When will I meet him?'

Grandma knew that his holidays would be over in a few weeks, and

Suman would come to take him back. But she determinedly refused to think about that future. That night when the phone rang, Amit ran to pick it up—there was so much to tell Mamma. 'Hello, Mamma?' he started and stopped when he heard a man's voice at the other end. 'Grandma, it's a call for you,' he said and disappeared to read his book. Grandma had guessed that it was Uday. 'Ma, who was that on the phone just now?' asked Uday, sounding slightly shocked as if he had guessed the answer! Grandma narrated all the events of the past few days while she only heard 'hmmm' from the other side from time to time. Uday didn't have anything to say in the end. He simply enquired about her health and bid bye—which disappointed Grandma greatly. She thought in stunned disbelief, 'Doesn't he even wish to talk to his son?'

She didn't know whether to worry about Uday or be angry with him. But she decided to push the incident to the back of her mind. 'I am going to enjoy my days with Amit and not waste them worrying about the mess that Uday has made of his life,' she told herself as she went looking for Amit. Luckily, Amit hadn't guessed who the caller was and looked immersed in his storybook.

The next day, Suman phoned to inform that she would be coming in a week to pick up Amit. After Amit had chatted to his heart's content, he gave the phone to Grandma. Suman could not hold back her feelings and said to Grandma, 'Ma, Amit sounds so happy! I am glad I decided to bring him to you. Will you forgive me for keeping both of you away from each other for so many years? I should not have allowed my differences with Uday to ruin your relationship.' Grandma assured her and her heart was filled with hope, as she hung up the phone. Suman's words meant that she would meet them on a regular basis now—'Perhaps Amit could spend most of his holidays with her in the future too!' She hummed a tune as she cooked their meal that evening!

Barely a day had passed when one late night, the doorbell rang. Grandma awoke with a start. 'Who could it be at this unearthly hour?'

she thought and couldn't decide whether to open the door or not. Just then, she thought she heard Uday's voice, 'Ma, it's me, Uday. Open the door.' She couldn't believe her ears and went closer to the door. When she heard Uday repeating his assurance as he knocked on the door this time, she rushed to open it quickly for him. Now she couldn't believe her eyes! It really was Uday—without any prior intimation and carrying just a small suitcase in his hand! 'Ma, Amit is still there with you, isn't he? I have come to meet him. I couldn't take a chance of waiting even for a few days in case he returned with Suman by then,' he rushed to say as he hugged her.

Grandma was overwhelmed and took him to the bedroom, where Amit was fast asleep. Uday lovingly gazed at his son and gave him a quick peck on his cheek so as to avoid disturbing him. He sat for a long time talking to Grandma, wanting to know everything about his son.

Amit woke up in the morning to have the most pleasant surprise of his life. He couldn't believe that he had his Papa with him! The initial shyness soon disappeared as the father-son duo spent time chatting about his school, friends and everything interesting that he had done with Grandma. The next few days were most joyful for both Amit and Grandma. 'To be in the company of your loved ones is bliss!' thought Grandma as she watched Uday and Amit concentrating on a game of chess. 'In another couple of days, Suman will be here too. With God's grace, when things have turned out so well so far, maybe Uday and Suman will be able to forget their differences and come back together! After all, 8 years have gone by since they separated from each other. And they both have had enough hard lessons of separation and loneliness,' Grandma mused wistfully.

While Grandma tucked Amit inside the sheets at night, she heard her thoughts being echoed by Amit! 'Grandma,' he said, 'Mamma too will be here soon. We will have more fun once Mamma also joins us.' And then he continued in a more serious tone, 'Grandma, do you think Mamma and Papa will start staying together again? I want all of us to be together—in India or Australia.' Grandma's eyes filled with tears as she assured him, 'Don't worry, Amit. I am sure Mamma and Papa will think about this. And both of us too will help them make the right decision—you persuade them with your love. And I will try to convince them like an adult—with lots of good advice and wisdom!'

Amit beamed with satisfaction as he closed his eyes.

Shadow

Vishakha Naware

I was happily looking at the sunset,
At the brilliant orange and red hues,
Beauteous, tranquil yet brazen,
Until she crept up on me.

I was happily looking at the birds on the treetop,
At the chirpy, twittery feathered wonders,
Wings in a flurry of motion,
Until she crept on me.

I was happily looking at the kite in the sky,
Intricate and appallingly swift,
Vivid colours splattered in the wild blue yonder
Until she crept on me.

She crept on me so stealthily,
Like a cat trying to sneak in for milk,
Like seagulls stealing bread from picnickers,
Her nefarious hands trying to engulf,
My innocent happiness!

The shadow of grief wants me,

To curl inside her,

To forget what my life means,

To mull over every mistake,

That I have made in my life.

Shadow of sorrow wants me,

To mourn every incompetence of mine,

To mourn every loss I ever had.

I look at her with conviction,

I know that shadows follow you everywhere,

They cannot be avoided, never ever!

I look at her confidently and say:

'You and I, dear grief, have to learn to coexist,

'Cause without you, I will never know,

The true meaning of life and happiness.'

Walk Away

Carol Mitra

I have been walking in a dark cave,

For quite a long time,

Never felt more caged and jailed,

As if I've committed a heinous crime!

Demons live under the beds they say,

You live in the house and come,

To my bed every day,

It's much more than what you tear away!

I closed my eyes to what I felt and saw,

Defeated and bruised, I stood up,

And walked to that door,

Hurt slowly seeping out of my core!

The knife digging into my spirit,

Threatening to pierce my soul,

I choose not to ignore it anymore,

Strength, I carry with a patient heart.

I now chose to make a brand-new start,
Those who suffer have an eye for suffering,
I've come to understand life is an exchange,
You lose something, and yet you gain.

That's a simple deal,
But no one tells you what to do,
Till you stand up from,
The shame you feel and walk away!

If At All You Knew!

Supraja Raghuram

The worth of words in a sentence,
The emotions that run behind the pretence.

The faith and trust that were supposed to be true,
I wish I could ask, if at all you knew?

For the tides and waves that sunk through the water,
The tears of joy that turned into laughter.

The unsaid and unheard words that were few,
I wish I could ask, if at all you knew?

The lights in the dark brightened our day,
The mystical breeze that made each of us sway,

Together, it was about the world in a drop of dew,
I wish I could ask, if at all you knew.

The spaces and the time changed forever,
The bond that it was couldn't have broken ever.

Explanations and expectations that are still due,
I only wish... I could ask if at all you knew!

Life is a Camera

Revathi Bhasker

Sumana had reported to the branch just that morning on transfer from the Local Head Office. Her transfer was on compassionate grounds as she was nursing her baby. There were many applications for transfer and her case was put through, superseding them, just because the Personnel Manager's wife was a close friend of hers. When the news of her transfer spread like wildfire, the Staff Association had almost staged a *dharna*, but fortunately for her, the Personnel Manager had issued the instructions just the day before he was transferred, and it could not be undone. However, she could sense the animosity written largely in the faces of others.

She was posted on the heaviest desk and not briefed at all about how to go about it. The nature of work in the Head Office and branches are entirely different, but since there was no support forthcoming from the branch staff, she tried to learn the ropes, though the hard way. The first day was really tough and it was nearly seven when she reached the creche to take her baby home. Regretting the delay and avoiding the steely glance of the caretaker, she left for home.

Her husband, Suyash, had not come home yet. Hurriedly she changed the baby's nappy and fed her and put her to bed. As she entered the kitchen, Suyash was at the door. He had brought a pizza for their dinner. He said that he had checked with his friend in her branch and came to know all that happened there. Suyash too worked in the same bank but in a different branch. In fact, he had met her at the Training Centre and fallen head over heels in love with her. It was not smooth sailing but somehow the parents came around and their patience paid off. During their two years courtship, they came to know each other very well and were very sure that theirs would be a 'made for each other' match. Both were at the Head Office occupying seats opposite each other, but after their wedding, they could not be in the same department. Sumana was first posted in a different department and after their baby was born got the posting to a branch closer home.

Suyash was a very efficient worker and Sumana held him in high esteem. He was in the Cash Department, but he knew all the accounting procedures thoroughly. Though Sumana was no less intelligent, they had decided that only one of them would appear for promotional examinations so that they could balance career and family well. Sumana readily agreed to look after the home and Suyash got promoted.

By the time Aaina was two years old, Suyash had risen in the ranks and was posted as the Chief Manager of a branch in the hilly areas. It was a two-year assignment and Sumana rose to the occasion. She managed her home and office well and also devoted quality time to Aaina. Suyash would come home every alternate weekend, but after a couple of months, the frequency reduced and sometimes he would be home only once in three months and that too for a day. When home, Suyash was the loving husband and doting father and Sumana did not note anything amiss. When Suyash was posted in the hills, they had come to an understanding that Sumana would meet household expenses from her salary and Suyash would save his. It worked well as Sumana efficiently managed the home.

It was now time to admit Aaina to a school. When Suyash was home that month, Sumana had asked him to remit Rs. 1 lac for donation to the school and admission fees, but even though a fortnight had passed, there was no money forthcoming. One evening when Sumana was slightly free, she went to the bank's website and logged into their joint account. What she saw was something she could not believe—the account had a balance of Rs. 0.60! She immediately called up Suyash. It was long before the call was answered. 'Hello,' cooed a very sweet voice. Sumana was stunned and did not know how to react. *'Saabji, koi phone pe hai'* (Sir, there is someone on the phone), she heard the woman say and waited for Suyash to come online. *'Boli kyun nahin ke saab busy hai?* (Why didn't you tell them that sir is busy),' came his reply. Sumana then disconnected.

Her thoughts ran wild. The phone call spoke volumes and explained Suyash's recent indifference. She then called up a common friend but when he did not pick up the phone, she walked down to his flat which was just a few blocks away. He had avoided picking up her phone but never imagined that she would personally call on him. Children were playing and as the door was open, Srikant could not avoid her.

Sumana did not beat about the bush and broached the topic straightaway. He did not hide anything from her. Suyash had stopped talking with him and his other friends when they came to know that he had gotten into bad company. They came to know that the village Pradhan's daughter had got very close to him. The Pradhan took advantage of this relationship and got all kinds of spurious loans sanctioned to his kith and kin. The loan accounts were getting irregular and Suyash was heading for trouble. Sumana could not listen any further. She merely stared at him for a while. Her silence was eloquent. She did not approve of such friends who would try to shield a person who was in the wrong. As his wife, Sumana needed to be informed and deserved to know the truth.

Sumana was disturbed and shattered, no doubt, but made up her mind that she would not crumble. She had read that we need to see life like a camera. We have within us the ability to focus, capture, develop and start all over if need be. We need to choose what is best so that we can focus on it, aim and shoot. Similarly, in life, we need to sift through all the clutter, meaningless things and relations in order to get a clear picture of what we would love to cherish, and which will be the very purpose of our existence. Nobody is perfect, but by focusing well and adjusting the settings properly, a picture-perfect is assured!

Once she was home and Aaina had gone to bed, she looked up her bank balance. Her salary was sufficient for her monthly maintenance, but it was Aaina's schooling that needed to be provided for. She sat with her laptop and the first thing she did was to ensure that Suyash had no access to her accounts by changing the passwords. She knew that he could wield influence in her branch and arrange to get money transferred from her account as it was a joint account. She drew up a letter to the Branch Manager to change the mode of operation from Either or Survivor to Former or Survivor, so that he would not be able to operate the account. If the Branch Manager insisted that this could be done only on the request of both parties, she thought she would confide in him the reason and he should normally consider her request as a genuine one and do the needful.

The next morning, she emptied the contents of the locker and applied for a loan against her ornaments. Then she listed all the investments she had made under the Income Tax Saving Schemes and calculated how much she would get if she were to redeem some of them. A rough calculation showed that she could raise about Rs.10 lac easily. Her Provident Fund could be used as a last resort, but this sum should be sufficient to see her through the crisis.

She applied for a week's leave and both mother and daughter drove down to the nearby Valley school. One of her bank clients was working in the school and she met her and sought admission for Aaina both in the school and hostel. On the way to the school, she had already mentally prepared Aaina who was quick to understand. Once the admission process was completed, they returned home to purchase all that was needed as well as to pack her things. They had a week before them and Sumana utilised her leave well.

Suyash had not bothered to return her call. His parents came one day to find out about him. Sumana curtly told them that he had not been in touch with her for quite a while and did not even bother about Aaina's school admission. She hinted that all was not right and that she regretted that they were not a 'made for each other' couple at all. Sumana's parents were living with her brother in the United States and Sumana did not wish they should know about these developments and get stressed. She was capable of facing the problems herself.

The school opened and Aaina seemed to like and get adjusted to the new surroundings. Periodically, Sumana would speak to her friend who was Aaina's local guardian. In the meanwhile, a new officer was posted at Sumana's branch and was on the lookout for a house to shift his family. Just a few days before, applications were invited from the staff to serve as Branch Inspectors and their assistants. For the first time, the Bank was offering these posts to women too.

Sumana instantly applied for it and told the new officer that in case she got selected, he could take her house on rent. Within a few days, news came that Sumana was selected and would need to attend the training in a fortnight's time in Jaipur. Once she was absorbed in the inspection and Audit department, she would have to be moving from place to place. As soon as she got the confirmatory letter, she gave her fully furnished house on lease to the Bank's officer.

While everything seemed to fall into place for Sumana, Suyash was in deep trouble. The irregularities in his branch could not be kept a secret forever. Once the NPAs (Non-Performing Assets) started rising and the branch was facing losses, an audit team descended on the branch and one by one everything was exposed. It was just a matter of days before he would be charge-sheeted and suspended. When he knew he was cornered, he called Sumana to tell her his predicament and that he would be home soon.

Sumana listened to him very patiently and then told him that the house was not with her anymore. She had entered into a lease agreement with the Bank. She also told him in no uncertain terms that she had married him, having loved and understood him, but he had not reciprocated it at all. His waywardness and squandering all his money, not even discharging his responsibility to his daughter and family had all taken a toll. She had already applied for a divorce, and he would soon be receiving the notice. 'You have been so absorbed in your own *leelas* (antics) that you don't even care to know what is going on. I had dreamt of a loving family, but you have shattered my dreams. Your parents had come enquiring about you. They may probably help you, but I regret I shall not be able to extend any kind of support. I have fixed my target and am focusing all my attention and efforts on reaching my goals. Soon, God willing, I will come up in life step by step as I am nurturing a hope that I will one day succeed, and Aaina will be proud of me. While I am confident that my *Esperanza* will be fulfilled, I am not too sure of yours!'

A Beholder's Burden

Mallika Chandrasekhar

I carry a beholders' burden,

A witness to your life,

Your struggles and strife.

The nights you spent crying,

Bereft, broken, alone,

It weighs me down,

To see you so low.

A life that has never been seen or felt,

A mother's love, a father's pride,

Sibling warmth, family joys,

You were unfairly neglected,

You were constantly negated.

Once a child of hope and laughter,

Now you're just a shadow of yourself,

I have seen you fight through it all!

An unhappy marriage,

To a nice man but a difficult husband,

I bore witness to those painful failed attempts,

At conceiving for seven years,

The depths of despair,

The terrifying sense of hopelessness,

Finally, mixed emotions when you did become a mother.

Wondering and doubting with fear and fright,

Whether you'd be good at your new role,

Would you be alright, would you do what's right?

I saw you suffer in silence,

Struggle with endurance,

The one thing that kept you strong, going on,

Was your incredible resilience.

To get up after every fall,

To rise higher after every painful descent,

There were times you were so close,

To giving in, giving up,

I witnessed those long spells of depression,

Willing and wishing you'd come around,

When you did it was such a proud moment,

Your indomitable spirit,

Ensured you returned back,

Stronger, wiser,

More determined to do, be better.

I may have felt weighed down,

By this beholder's burden of your life,

But I am also immensely proud and honoured,

To bear witness to your amazing strength and courage.

As your shadow, I know you like no other,

As your witness, I decree you a warrior like none other!

Garden—A Metaphor for Hope

Mallika Chandrasekhar

Plant a seed,

Sow a thought,

Pull out the weeds,

Pluck the flowers,

Arrange a posy,

Pick out the fruits,

Tend to the soil,

Harvest hope and cheer,

Be close to the earth,

Nurture nature,

Be nourished by her.

Watch it grow,

From seed to sapling,

To flowers and fruits,

Observe the sprout,

Acknowledge the results,

Of your thoughts and actions.

Fertilise it with your imagination,

Show it graciously,

Your bountiful garden,

Share it generously,

Your hope and haven.

Remember life's greatest joys,

Comes from sharing what you create,

A garden is about hope and abundance,

It is also about giving and sharing.

For life becomes beautiful and meaningful,

When you sow, grow, give and share,

A garden of flowers and fruits,

And a heart full of love and hope,

So, expand your heart ceaselessly,

Till your garden, grow in hope,

Give it willingly,

Share it lovingly.

Love Anyway

Mallika Chandrasekhar

Love is sometimes undeclared,

You love anyway.

Love is not always demonstrated in a drama or in words,

You love anyway.

Love is not Valentine's celebration or gifts of red roses,

You love anyway.

Love is not always dreams fulfilled and aspirations met,

You love anyway.

Love is not always songs of spring and dances under the rain,

You love anyway.

Love is sometimes sudden tragedy and loss of hope,

You love anyway.

Love is sometimes subtle signs and surreptitious looks,

You love anyway.

Love is not overt expressions or expected experiences,

You love anyway.

Love is not always a love story, but a story of love,

You love anyway.

Love is not always traditions and togetherness,

You love anyway.

Love is sometimes short-lived like the season of coral jasmine flowers,

You love anyway.

Love is sometimes just an unexplainable distance. And sudden death,

You love anyway.

Love is more than the visible, expressional aspect of emotion,

Love is a silent covenant between the heart and soul of one to the heart and soul of the other,

You love anyways because love is not dependent on the existence of the person loved,

But on the willingness of the person who loves to keep loving.

Hope Led Me Back to Myself

Dinaz Treger-Patel

The part where you get to know the author

How does one begin to write their own story? This is a question I have always had whenever I read a book in the most uncomfortable position and at the untimeliest hour that is known to any bookworm on the face of this planet.

I guess instead of staring at my laptop, hoping that words would magically bounce from my head and arrange themselves neatly in sentences; I'll write about my story with as much honesty as I can.

Do note—This is not your usual story that has been mostly showcased in multiple Bollywood and/or Hollywood movies where the guy falls in love with the girl head over heels and after the 'meet, greet and dance phase,' some tragedy happens and boom—the girl ends up with someone else, leaving this guy in a full-fledged Kabir Singh/ Devdas kind of heart-broken way (rolls her eyes).

No! This story is different!

Because this story is of a girl who once believed in love.

She was kind, gentle, and warm, with an infectious optimistic energy sprinkled with a great (and sometimes lame) sense of humour, and a heart that would always try to see the "good" in a person.

This is the story of a girl who fell for a guy. He later cheated on her with someone else and got married to that person.

Uh-oh! Is it too soon to reveal the ending? Well, that is what happened and if you would stick around for a while with me, I would like to invite you to witness her journey through her eyes.

The part where I write about my past

One moment can change it all.

You never know how a single moment could be so important in your life until you look back at that very specific moment in your mind. Don't you agree?

Well, that's what happened to me when I locked eyes with the guy whom I met for the first time. This is the moment where it all began.

Let me take you on a quick trip down my memory lane.

We stayed in touch via social media and met after quite a few months for the first time. He listened, I talked, and the evening flew by in an instant. I felt calm with him and comfortable enough to open up about myself layer by layer.

The first couple of years with him were beautiful with their own fair share of ups and downs. We would talk about our future goals and spend time knowing about each other.

One of my mottos that I live by is—I don't want to die with regrets; the regrets of not doing something that my heart was into, and that made me take the risk to propose to this guy.

Well, even after that proposal, things "seemed" okay. However, the problem began when he started hiding things from me. We would sit together yet feel miles apart. We would fight, yell and scream more than we used to love, listen and hug each other.

The mess began when he was already seeing someone else. The thought of him looking at someone the way he once used to look at me broke something deep inside my heart.

We had broken up emotionally way before he ended things by sharing about his marriage with the girl he was secretly seeing.

To be honest with you, I had sensed that long back, too. Looking back, I realise I wasn't courageous enough to walk away. (Sighs deeply.)

The part where I write about anger

Furious, irate, seething, infuriated, livid, incandescent, wrathful, murderous; be it any synonym of the word "anger", I was feeling all of them in their highest intensity.

I remember drowning myself in questions such as:

'Why would he do that to me?' and the classic 'What did I do wrong?'

Yes! The voices in my head went bonkers and I felt I was about to breathe fire like a Drogon! (Daenerys Targaryen's *Dragon. Game of Thrones* fans assemble!)

This part was the heaviest for me to go through because I did not know what to do with all of this anger within me. I was angry at him for many things and angry at myself as well.

I would cry my eyes out. There were times when I screamed my heart out by stuffing my face in the pillow. I felt lost, stuck, and broken.

Mostly, I had lost hope.

The part where I write about silence

No one talks about the phase where you're feeling so bone-deep tired that uttering a single word when someone asks you if you're okay, seems next to impossible. After my anger episodes decreased in intensity, I slipped into the phase of being emotionally numb to any outer situations and/or my inner feelings.

I knew what I was feeling and the cause. However, the moment anyone would ask about how I was doing, I would freeze for a second. I felt all the languages leaving my brain. I would think of a satisfactory response but would end up saying, 'It's nothing.'

It breaks my heart a little when I see this version of myself. The once talkative girl just sitting there in silence all by herself, contemplating over all the negative things that had happened to her till she could physically feel the pain in every inch of her skin and eventually drift off to sleep.

The part where I talk about grief

Grief is a strange emotion.

I became familiar with this emotion during my 'lay down in bed and stare at the ceiling' phase which followed for two weeks after things had completely ended between us.

I understood (or tried to make sense of) how grief is not only experienced when a loved one dies.

I was grieving

~ about the life I will not have with him and the family that I thought we'll have.

~ about all the things that I left unsaid, thinking, and hoping that there will be a better time to say them.

~ about the self that I lost on the way when I was becoming someone else for him, hoping that he would find a way to stay with me.

~ about the memories that were slowly fading, clashing, collapsing, and dying inside my mind.

~ about all the list of places I had made that I wanted to visit with him and the memories we could have made while we were there together.

And when I sat upright to wipe the tears that wouldn't stop rolling down my cheeks, did I realise that I was grieving about the person I had become and was questioning who I am.

Grief, indeed, is a strange emotion.

The part where I talk about my "oops" and my "takeaways"

When I look back at my relationship (or the lack of it), I saw how I played my part in the gradual decay and death of this relationship with my partner and that was a bitter pill for me to swallow.

I would like to share some of my **"*oops*"** with you here.

About how—

~ I built my world around him.

~ I kept seeking external validation; someone to tell me that 'I was enough.'

~ I wanted him to be versus seeing him as he had become and because of that discrepancy, I was brewing a recipe of unhappiness within myself.

~ I ended up (imagine a clingy, conscious, insecure version of me here who would crave for external validation)

versus

~ how I used to be when I first met him (imagine a confident, happy-go-lucky, sassy version of me here).

And once I accepted these "oops" of mine, I also made a note of my

"takeaways".

About how to—

~ Keep me as the topmost priority. Unapologetically!

~ Honour my self-respect.

~ Accept and love myself unconditionally and know it into being that 'I Am Enough'.

~ Draw healthy boundaries.

~ Cut ties (gently but firmly) that are not being maintained by both people involved.

~ Stay my best, authentic self.

The part where I talk about forgiveness

When I write about forgiveness, I do not wish to write only about forgiving the other person.

More importantly, I write about forgiving yourself for:

~ each time you said "yes" when you wanted to say "no".

~ all the false hopes you gave yourself about your significant person.

~ ignoring the red flags of your relationship.

~ all the wrong things you said when you were angry.

~ not knowing that you deserved better at certain points in your life.

~ not respecting yourself enough to walk away from people who hurt you.

~ for messing things up that the grief still haunts you.

~ for the darker and shadowed parts of you.

~ all the versions you couldn't become.

The part where I talk about the process of healing

The healing process comes in waves and goes in waves. On some days you might feel you're over that pain, healed and doing great. On the other days, you'll feel miserable, hopeless, angry and unmotivated.

I learned how healing never was and never will be linear. I learned that there is always a *choice*, and I knew that's where my power is.

I *chose* to go through those messy, uncomfortable days and nights by journaling about it and making peace with that part of my life. It wasn't comfortable and honestly, it definitely wasn't pretty.

I *chose* to seek closure from my end instead of numbing the pain by pouring myself into academics and/or work.

I *chose* not to neglect what happened. I gradually accepted that what happened was horrific, terrible, and utterly disheartening and *choose* to also cherish the good times that we had together.

It feels amazing to share with you that through journaling and many other ways, I have been able to make peace not only with myself but also with him (in my mind) and the entire event.

The part where I talk about hope

Another spoiler alert—It does get better with time; I can assure you that!

You will feel so incredibly alive again like man oh man your cheeks will hurt from smiling and those days WILL come in your life.

You know, there are still some days where I feel down in the dumps; whereas, on other days, I'll be dancing and prancing my way through the day.

Because there's one thing that I've learned from observing my journey that I'd love to share with you.

'Sometimes you tend to think so much about what happened, or fear about what might happen, that you actually are missing the life that's passing you by this very moment.'

Read it again slowly and let each word sink within.

When I bring my attention to where my hands are, THAT is where my life is happening; as my Guru would say: *'In the here and now.'*

I'd love to quote Ferris Bueller (from the movie Ferries Bueller's Day Off) here with a slight moderation: *'If I don't stop and look around once in a while at my life, I could miss it.'*

The part where I talk about new beginnings

In the beginning did you notice the line where I wrote that this story is about a girl who once believed in love?

Well, Good news! She's not someone who "once believed", but rather still believes in love.

She's found joy in creating happiness and peace within her that she once was looking outside of her.

She's still someone who sees and appreciates the good in people.

She trusts to meet a person who will hold her hand while they walk together, meets her gaze, listens to her, showers her with forehead kisses and embraces her whenever he can.

She's learning, unlearning and relearning.

She's found the courage to open her heart to love again and begin a new chapter in her life.

She's found a way back to her.

And I'm here to tell you that if she can, so can **You!**

I hope you find the courage to open your heart and look for reasons that give you hope. I wish they arrive at you in the most serendipitous ways you had never even imagined.

I rest my pen (figuratively speaking) with a little smile playing on my face.

I hope whenever you come back and read my story, it strikes some chords in your heart and makes you believe in that little ray of sunshine called "Hope" that poets and writers write about.

Believe!

I Made a Quilt

Pushpa Bhatt

You left me in pieces,

When you broke my heart.

I was left holding a crumbling heart,

And now you will never be back.

I looked at my pale blue heart

And the gaping hole in it.

I knew I had to mend it,

But how do you mend a broken heart?

Too many broken pieces,

And do hearts mend?

Choking on a cry,

I said, let me at least try.

I put down all the broken pieces,

Clenching my lips,

It was one big mess,

But I didn't want to rest my case.

I sorted it slowly with hope,

I needed a strong rope,

So, I brought out the thread of memories,

And I fitted back all the pieces.

I sewed it tight into a colourful quilt,

It looked amazing with so many things,

There was one last piece,

The one that was missing.

I was confused and wondered,

Just then my heart expanded,

To fit the missing piece,

And it made me whole again.

The universe was happy that I tried,

Sky dropped a big Shining Star,

I put that shining star on top of my quilt,

My heart had never looked more exquisite.

If you close your eyes and touch my heart,

You will feel my scars and breaks,

A strong heart with creases,

Full of rich experiences.

It is a beautiful quilt,

Made of broken pieces,

Yes, in the end,

Hearts do mend.

Friends

Subhashree. S

In the world,

When you're alone,

And don't have anyone to share your sorrow,

Friends are always there when you need them.

When you look over your shoulder,

You do feel lonely,

A friend comes to your rescue,

And makes you feel pleasant as you were.

A friend shares happiness,

Helps you to break down the walls

And is on your side

When the times of toughness arrive.

Friends stay in your hearts always,

Even if you're far away,

Or they are away,

Always think of them and they'll be beside you.

Life was hard for me when I left my friend,

It made me feel lonely to resettle,

In the place I was born,

A new school, new friends and a new place to live,

Made me think my friends are without me.

I cried.

O! I cried day and night,

Longing for my friends,

To meet them, to see their happy faces,

To see them smile.

I resettled,

Moved on,

And decided,

It was time,

I made a set of new friends.

So, I did,

They indeed supported me

I felt happy, thinking of the first time I made friends,

At the same place after eight years.

Though I miss my friends,

And long to see them,

Under the shooting stars,

I made the wish.

That I will see them soon!

At times like this,

The lesson I learnt is that

True friendship never breaks,

Until you forget your true friends.

Fighter

Subhashree. S

Push me down,
This agonising cliff,
I'd rather fall,
Than you see me stiff.

I am a fighter,
Don't you understand?
I am here,
And here I stand.

I am the only one,
Who's the hero of my story,
I'd rather fight,
Than you let me down slowly.

I am here,

To save my house,

At any cost,

I'll chase you out, you mouse!

I am a fighter,

I am brave,

I am strong,

So go away!

The sun calls me,

And shimmers its rays,

And I fly there,

To burst into flames!

A Story of Courage, Patience and Hope

Dinaz Treger-Patel

Nocturnal Thoughts

Strobilanthes callosus (aka Karvi flowers in the Marathi language) bush takes seven years to mature. It doesn't begin to blossom until the eighth year. The shrub has a fascinating life cycle; it comes alive and green with the arrival of the monsoon every year, but after the rainy season is gone, all that is left are dried and dead-looking stems. This process continues for seven years before the plant erupts into mass blooming in the eighth year.

I was fortunate to witness the beauty of these when I went hiking at the Ratangad Fort in the month of October, 2022.

I'm on my way back home, taking memories and learnings in my bag from this journey. Certain parts of my body are aching, serving as a subtle reminder that this wasn't a dream, and I was really able to experience this beautiful phenomenon of Mother Nature.

I'm bone-deep tired and about to plop in my bed when my mind starts to open up and wander in the tranquillity of the night. It is in this very space of silence that I start to think about everything that happened to me and led me here to this very moment.

I was pondering about the similarities of how it took 7 years for me and my family to bloom like these *Karvi* flowers. How? you ask. Well, let me begin sharing my story with you by asking this simple question: What comes to your mind when you read the word 'family'?

My Family

For me, well, I've seen my family being tight and by each other's sides when I was a little kid. My uncles and my dad laughing at the top of their voices, cracking the same old jokes; my elder cousins teaching me how to play cricket and PlayStation; roaming at Juhu beach and malls with my aunt and mom, days passing by in a jiff whenever we came here to Mumbai during my summer vacations.

That's what I see in my mind's eye. Until of course, one incident led to another, and chaos rained down.

Aren't I the dramatic one, eh? Well, why don't we make a quick journey to the past and take a glimpse? The story might have a heart-rending beginning, but I promise you one thing, it did get better.

I'm a die-hard Shah Rukh Khan fan and one of his dialogues that stuck with me is the one from the movie Om Shanti Om where he says:

'Aaj iss baat ka yakeen ho gaya, ki hamari filmon ki tarah humari zindagi mein bhi, end tak sab kuch theek-theek ho jaata hai. Happies Ending. Aur agar theek naa ho, toh woh 'The End' nahi. Picture abhi baaki hai mere dost.'

(A rough translation to this would be: Today I have come to believe that our life is also like our Hindi movies, where everything works out in the end. "A Happy Ending". But if all is not well, then it is not the end. The film isn't over yet, my friend.)

Shattered Dreams

Let me take you to the very beginning, where it all began in the year 2015, when we shifted from Surat to Mumbai. My mom decided to have us a better education (by us I mean my younger brother and myself). I was excited to pursue my graduation in the city of dreams.

Talking about dreams, I too, had a long list of my own:

~Explore the city and travel outside as well.

~Learn how to ride a bike (Royal Enfield to be specific).

~Join Shiamak Davar's Dance Academy.

~Hit the gym, learn how to swim, paint, and on and on.

In a nutshell, I wanted to do all this and so much more. These are just few of many dreams that I had scribbled in my diary.

Imagine an excited version of me here, will you? Eyes full of hopes, dreams, and contagious optimism.

Because after a week, everything that I ever had and desired to have, was going to be snatched away right in front of my eyes. And the worst part—we had never even imagined that our own family members would play the key role in causing this havoc.

Hey! Psst! Before you go on in my journey, spoiler alert—the version of me that you just imagined above was lost somewhere miserably. However, the one thing that I did not lose was the hope that I carried in my heart, no matter how, at times, small the light would be.

The Domino Effect

It's almost heartbreakingly funny how my memories of this event are blurred to an extent where I'm unable to articulate the perfect chronology of the events and yet the emotions that are rising within my chest are as fresh as if I came out of that fight a moment ago.

Yes. A fight. That's how it all began.

You see, my mom's younger brother (let's call him Kans) was supportive in the beginning, or that's what we thought, when we moved from another state. A week later he created a ruckus in the lobby of the building where he pushed me and my mom outside the house, claiming this flat is his and we weren't welcome anymore.

Half the time I was screaming back at Kans and the other half of me was too shocked to make any sense of this nonsense. I had never seen this side of him, and I saw all of my dreams collapse, bit by bit, in front of my eyes. This lasted for about an hour or so until my mom decided to give a call to her elder sister.

The Aftermath

To cut a long story short, let me share some highlights that followed post that fight—

1. My uncle (mom's brother-in-law; let's call him Uncle J) was kind enough to give us space in his apartment (which was next door), so that our studies wouldn't be affected. From living in a spacious two-storied bungalow in Surat, to a one-room flat was the first punch that life hit me in the guts with.

2. There was no TV and no cupboards in that flat. My clothes remained in one large travel bag, one suitcase and one mini travel bag, till this drama of mine ended in January 2022.

3. From watching movies on a big screen to watching them on our mobile phones (at least till I got a laptop which didn't happen so soon either), was the second punch in my face.

4. My mom and her sister (let's call her Aunt K) tried to sort this feud through amicable means. They would give in to all of Kans' illogical demands just to maintain peace within the family. Did it work? No, sadly it didn't.

5. A lawyer was hired, a case was lodged in the court and with that went my mom's savings, my dad's contribution from his monthly pension, my mom's, my brother's and my gold jewellery.

For my friends, weekends meant relaxing, partying, going to new places; whereas for me it was going to the lawyer's office, drafting letters, and arguing with Kans whenever he would threaten or frighten my family.

A part/full-time job requires commitment and time; with things being almost completely uncertain at my end, I couldn't walk down that path as well and hence decided to keep my head in the books and simultaneously focus on getting a way out of this rathole.

6. My mom got hospitalised in 2016, the underlying cause was her being completely stressed out about everything that had been going on. I missed my college and tuition and that's when my teachers came to know what I was going through. I was the smart, happy-go-lucky, helpful student in my college whose only aim was to get her name on the list of toppers on the wall of her college.

7. The months of monsoon were dreadful for us. A sudden downpour would flood our house in the middle of the night, and we'd have to shift all our belongings from the floor to the bed, sit for the next 7 hours until the water drained from the houses, followed by cleaning the mess that it left behind, causing complete physical and mental agony.

Phew!! Quite the roller coaster ride, isn't it?

If it's okay, I would like to show you the view through my eyes.

Rekindled Hope

Johan Cruyff, a Dutch football player and coach, once said, *'Every disadvantage has an advantage.'* Quite beautiful, isn't it? And I could relate to it as well.

If you could be so kind as to read one point from the list above and then one from the list below, you'll see how I started looking at my situation from a different perspective. It'll be fun.

1. ***On the upside,*** I slowly and gradually learned how to manage within small spaces and got comfortable in it as well.

2. ***On the upside,*** I learned the importance of buying only what is necessary. I started asking myself the question whenever I felt the desire to buy things that weren't necessary: *'Do I really need it, or do I just want it?'*

3. ***On the upside,*** it didn't matter much later because I had my pile of books to the rescue. I was away from the gossip and more focused on shaping my own world. I started spending more time with my family, plus could fill my days with activities such as painting, cooking, and writing. I started practising meditation on a regular basis which helped me big time!

4. ***On the upside,*** I started observing and understanding people more than what they portrayed through the masks that they wear. I could see the potential dangers that financial matters could bring into one's family and learning from that, I consciously started having mature conversations with my brother on how we could decide not to repeat the same in our lives in the future.

5. ***On the upside,*** I learned how to communicate, negotiate and be assertive in situations that even, at times, the elders were not able to do themselves. Because I couldn't work, I found out about a Diploma course as an Integrative Counsellor, and I found my calling in the field of Mental Health as a psychologist.

6. ***On the upside,*** I started appreciating my days, my health, and would share my thoughts about it with the people who were in touch with me. I started valuing how short life is; that in turn made me take chances and not live in regret. I learned to let go

of certain things/ events, was able to (and still am trying my best) forgive more, love more, and try my best to maintain certain close relations.

7. ***On the upside,*** I could see how resilient humans can be, even and especially in, their toughest times. I started being more grateful towards life and still continue the same. This reminds me of Robin William's dialogue from one of my all-time favourite movies Good Will Hunting: *'You'll have bad times, but it'll always wake you up to the good stuff you weren't paying attention to.'*

To Hope and Happy Beginnings

Yes, you read it right. Happy beginnings.

I feel immensely grateful to write that the matter that dragged on for so long did come to an end.

I fell down and I got back up, I laughed, and I cried, I stumbled, fumbled, jumbled up, messed up, learned and am still learning.

I do look back and think about how my life would be if this event never happened. Where would I be right now, if I had gone to Deutschland to pursue my MBA?

Of course, I do NOT end up feeling quite good at the moment and at that time I remind myself of Arthur's dialogue (from the movie Passengers) that brings me back to the here and now:

'You can't get so hung up on where you'd rather be that you forget to make the most of where you are. Take a break from worrying about what you can't control. Live a little.'

(YES! I'm a cinephile! You guessed it right!)

I can say that everything did work out in the end. My life didn't turn out as I had expected or dreamed of or desired and yet I'm hopeful & eager to embrace life's challenges & surprises.

And I hope, YOU, the one reading this, find the courage and hope within you as well when things don't seem to work in your favour.

I'd love to thank you for walking with me through this journey and saying "*Auf Wiedersehen*" instead of a dramatic "Goodbye".

There is this beautiful quote from the movie *Shawshank Redemption* by Andy Dufresne that I would love to leave you with:

'Hope is a good thing, maybe the best of things, and no good thing ever dies.'

Gift of Pandora

Shivali Singh

Stoned eyes, her face was paler,
The visible wounds, just a trailer.
Her faint smile desperately trying to hide,
The bleeding wounds embedded inside.

She had numbed the pain, time and again,
Shutting her eyes, clotting the blood in her vein.
Glorious past driving her insane!
Conviction to hold on clouding her brain.

With Aphrodite's blessings and by God himself,
She'd received the nectar and ambrosia.
How could she lose? Walk out by herself,
She was stoned by the law of inertia.

She had opened the box of Pandora,
And treasured the hope inside.
Extending her suffering, denying her aura,
The gift of Zeus, wrath for mankind.

She dreamt of birds soaring high with might,
Dreamt of blooming flowers that night.
Her sun-kissed wounds, washed off by drops of dew,
She was healed to the core shining new.

She now saw herself in the new light,
Freed from the self-held bondage.
Took the step forward with brave insight,
Holding the treasured hope within the package.

The gift enclosed in the Pandora,
Is in itself mighty and strong,
Never use it to hold you back,
It's your shield as you rewrite your song.

You Are Not Alone

Mallika Chandrasekhar

You are not alone,

In your fight and struggle,

To feel safe, to stay sane.

Remember, everyone is fighting a battle,

Of some kind or the other.

The only difference is that

Each of us is fighting it,

At different battlegrounds,

In different time zones.

I understand how you're,

Fighting and feeling right now,

Low, depressed, and despairing,

Believe me, I know intimately how it feels,

As if the fire in the soul has died down,

Bereft of reasons to carry on,

Is your mind playing tricks?

Are your emotions playing truant?

Yeah, I know it feels crazy and chaotic,

But believe me, when I tell you,

You're not alone.

There are thousands of others feeling the same thing,

I don't know how this will make you feel better,

But just knowing that you're not alone,

That someone somewhere is feeling just as wretched as you.

That if you try to make it through the next moment,

So will the other unknown stranger,

Struggling with the same chaos and confusion as you.

So, cry if you have to,

Scream if you have to,

Punch a wall too,

But keep reminding yourself,

That you are not alone,

Neither in your sorrow nor in your joy.

Giving Up Is Not an Option

Mallika Chandrasekhar

Life may have handed you,

Some tough lessons and

Hard choices.

It may have thrown you,

In the deep end of,

Life experiences filled with challenges.

It may have served up,

Human relationships abounding with indifference,

You may have had to work harder than most others,

Either to prove your worth,

Or negate negative impressions,

You may have had,

No sense of protection,

Or the idea of self-preservation.

Plenty of drawbacks giving you company,

Personality, physicality, and abilities,

Many disadvantages and difficulties,

May have been your lot in life,

You may have felt like giving up the fight.

Giving in to the utter madness within,

The demonic mind convinced that others are right,

There's something not good and right about you,

The broken heart though persistently conveying,

That love will triumph overall.

You may be torn between two weak choices,

You may have at some point in time,

Succumbed to the demons in the mind,

Barely making it back to sanity and a clear sense.

You may have had to lie, decide,

Between a rock and a hard place,

Both alternatives distraught,

You may be struggling,

Every moment of every day,

Being resilient, becoming strong,

Sell- improving personal aspects,

Ascending to a higher self, spiritually evolving,

Remaining positive, being loving,

Wondering if it all really matters,

Does it matter?

Do you matter?

To anyone?

But then there's a tiny voice,

A squeak actually,

Like a flutter of a butterfly's wing,

Or a soft birdsong whispering,

"Giving up is not an option,

Giving up is not an option."

Phoenix and the Devil

Srishti Sareen

From the ages when all wars had sharpened stones and poisonous arrows. To the point where we all are right now, in the current era. In the era where every territory marked or unmarked has excellence in arms and ammunition. We have worked hard to accomplish something beyond authority and ownership. But still, what is the main purpose of life? What is the reality of our existence? Are weapons the only thing we need? Do our souls focus on weapons and armour only? Is it sufficient? Will it ever be sufficient? Is it true that all a human being needs for its survival is ammunition? What if it isn't? What if all one needs is hope?

Hope to find the strength to love the unlovable, find calm in chaos, forgive the unforgiven, and hug the one whose mere touch feels like salt to your wounds. What humans need in their life is just to feel human again. Feel normal and warm, in a place that doesn't seem like home.

But normalcy is a myth. What is life if it's normal? Day in and day out no discrepancies, cuts, or bleeds. Just a bowl of bland almond oatmeal. Life only feels alive when its toxicity is off the charts. The moment your brain goes into the messed-up moments. The reality of life. When one accepts the facts and figures. When life is not all black and white. This is the moment when one's life is beyond rainbows and butterflies. It is unimaginably heart-wrenching and painful when things are not in your hands.

That's what life is, the bittersweet syrup with drops of Wolfsbane. Moments when every headache scares you. Every scar brings you down to the day when you willfully pressed the wrong breaks. Because blood thickens and one's breath is questionably denser. There are fears you don't want to narrate because if you do your palms will sweat and bones will be stiff for no damn reason. The first box on your list will be ticked off. Slowly and slowly, you will know how lightly you took those 60 to 100 heartbeats you have in a minute.

Life should be feared because what your first headache really was or what it could be was and always will be a mystery. You will never realise how a random night could be your only night. You will never know what it feels like when you fear closing your eyes living under the same roof confided in the same four walls. Because there is always the horror of darkness boiling up in your blood about what if there is a moment when you do close your eyes, but they just won't open. And in case they do, you will lose yet another twelve days of your life, wiped off clean. Your life is nothing but a loveless affair between your soul and the hole, you dug yourself for your grave.

You'll write stories, poems, and sonnets expressing the darkness of your life overpowering hope. Regardless of all this, there will be a story that will be closer to you than someone else. Because that story will be damned by the truths of your secrets. It will not even need to be structured by dialogues because somehow you won't need them. You won't need the foundation to be explanatory through the human voices. Because words will be enough for the validity of missing truths.

It was the first fall from the sky,

After so long, the barren land got its touch.

The drops of rain were all around on every existing atom of this world,

Over the red roses and even her fresh bare skin.

Everything was different and new, now,

The scent of the sky's first fall was raw and magical.

Even the droplets of rain had a little bit of snow and hellfire of their own.

They were fresh and shimmered like pearls falling from heaven.

Yet, they were salty and toxic.

The pearls were gifted to the banished phoenix of a land unknown by the devil himself,

The pearls she kept wrapped around her neck.

In hope of the salt to crystallise

Into something exotic

Which can never be used or touched but always be embraced in ways you never grazed.

But she clung to those pearls for so long,

Till her hands were numb.

Numb enough that it was hard for her to move,

She was unconscious now and was unaware of the crystallised salt.

She is now shackled, and her wrists have signs of struggle,

The struggle of clinging to the pearls she wrapped around her neck.

There was nothing left in her life other than imprints and dripping blood,

The wrists that were doomed to be in shackles till the hell breaks on earth.

Neither the bones were broken,

Nor were those wrists were unchained.

She died with a soft growl,

Thus, now untangled with broken chains.

Her struggle was of no use,

Now the pearls were stolen.

It was the first fall from the sky,

After so long, the barren land got its touch.

In a hope of fallen promises wrapped around the neck. It was prominent how everything was falling apart. Yet, it existed in the form of pain and sorrow.

Those four walls and roof over the head were once a room,

But not anymore.

Now it's mere cement, brick, and freckled paint,

But the furniture and centrepieces stayed the same.

The little machine to keep track of blood pressure is still there,

In the right corner of the counter.

Nothing changed,

But it is dusty.

The old man with white hair is not there anymore,

But the framed photograph is intact in the house.

Memories are nothing but just like burnt toast,

Hard to swallow the toast the moment it hits the taste buds.

The blurred smile

And hummed whispers are far gone.

Everything structured in someone's mind is nothing

But a crystal ball which just can't be understood,

Until cracked open.

But the fear one has is more questionable than opening that crystal ball,

It is the darker sharp ends and the mysterious reasons it beholds.

The white lies of being okay to be alive

And the almost forgotten bittersweet recollections,

Because just like his soul those recollections are fading away too.

No matter how much pain the heart swallows,

The bitterness of the void will always be alive.

Those four walls and roof over the head were once a room,

But not anymore.

Ray of Hope

Dimple Makkhija

Your glimpse is miles away,
Where thirsty souls meet.
The serenity of your touch sublimes my being
When the birds sing in effervescent glory.

I am inspired to love every time by my trampled heart,
Courage to still find you in my deepest oceanic being.
Always searching for signs,
Even while I live in a land of improbable dreams.

Providing me solace in the realm of your search,
Whilst I turn every page of my life,
To finding pleasures in small things,
Leading movement into moments.

Filled with joyous lyrical beauty,
My eyes still brim with emotion,
Carrying the depths of my deepest feelings,
In search of the ray of hope being you.

Optimism, Unlocked!

Tanushree Keshan

'Dream is not what you see in sleep.

A dream is something which doesn't let

you sleep.'

The line always gives me cold creeps,

And reminds me:

I always hope to fly in the sky with open wings and big dreams,

And in my mind, my goals always stream.

For, I promised myself to never look back, to never look down,

To never cry, and to always have a smile on my face instead of a
frown.

I was tired, and I thought of giving up midway,

But it was my passion and courage that kept me going throughout
the night and day.

The roads were not paved with gold,

It proved my struggle because those wicked ways were to be
moulded.

I never knew, but my struggles made me strong,

But with a smile on my face, and while singing a song, I managed to cross that road which was so long.

I kept taking baby steps,

And I never lost my confidence, even after falling into the biggest depth.

With a mind full of confidence, and a fire inside my heart,

I am ready to build my own empire using my art.

The Last Dance

Mallika Chandrasekhar

Have you ever witnessed,

A curtain of dry leaves,

Being blown by a gentle breeze?

Have you seen how they,

Dance before they touch the ground?

The last dance,

Is the one before vanishing.

Withering the last express life,

A twist, a twirl, a joyous swirl,

Leaves that accept the inevitable.

There's a sense of utter surrender,

When the dead dry leaves fall,

A gesture of a final farewell bid,

Before the descent with grace and graciousness,

Holding nothing back, submitting its everything.

Can you imagine us, humans, in the last dance?

Can we hope to beautifully choreograph?

Our final exit from existence?

With elegance and an evocative spirit?

Can we let go and let be like the leaves of the tree?

Being Late—A Blessing in Disguise

Sumakalyani Ganti

Ranjani had just come to the temple. It was a *Ganpati* temple, adjoining platform number 4 towards the east side of Mulund, a suburb in Mumbai. She was staying at Mulund West. Part of her daily routine was to cross the bridge every evening, come to this temple for the evening aarti, participate in this beautiful hymn to the Lord, wait for some time, sit on the pious temple floor for a while, align her thoughts and then slowly walk back home after taking darshan of her *Ganpati Bappa*. In the past few decades, He had always, on many occasions, managed to help her get to the shore. She often remembered *Sukhakarta dukhaharta* sung by Lata Mangeshkar. She had been gifted a two-in-one radio cum tape recorder by her brother, more than a decade ago, in the early 90s. But it was of good use. She had many recorded tapes, and one or the other devotional *bhajans* was always on the play, as long as she was in the kitchen.

The kitchen was where her fridge was. Her *bahar se chotta, andar se bada* Godrej refrigerator, just like her *ghar chhota, par dil bada wala* (house is small, but the heart is big) feeling was placed in the kitchen. The radio was kept on the fridge, and a small stack of cassettes too was placed to the side. There was a fridge cover, on the top, so as to prevent dust from accumulating. The embroidery on that, as she fondly used to remember every day, was made by her son Harish as part of his school craft curriculum during his middle school days, in his 8th grade. It was a very beautiful piece of art. Her son was a versatile person, even during his school days—A classical singer loved by the music department, an artist always loved by his art teacher, a helpful child, always ready to share his notes with his classmates, and an ever-helpful elder brother who mentored his little sister. A responsible child! People around her used to be jealous. She had put up this embroidered cloth as the fridge cover, and it had been there for years together now.

Ranjani had learnt a lesson of spirituality right from her childhood and had imbibed her mom's qualities of providing for everyone who was there at home and visited them too. She was habituated to chanting some shlokas all the while she was cooking. Since the time, the two-in-one was gifted to her, Harish recorded some of her favourite cassettes of *bhajans* and kept them for his mom. She believed that the essence of what she was doing entered the food that she was preparing, and the end result always had a glimpse of that. Every Thursday had *Sai Baba Aarti* at all four times of the day, while Tuesdays always saw Lata Didi's *Ganapati Bappa chi Aarti* humming in her kitchen. So, her belief that her cooking contained the essence of the Almighty always satisfied her.

It was almost a decade, in fact exactly ten years to the date that she had been visiting this temple almost every day. People knew her, expected her every day and she by herself knew that her *Bappa* was waiting for her every day. People could set their clocks, by her entry. Ranjani was very rich in virtues, and punctuality was one such trait. At sharp 6.30 pm, she would walk into the temple, come heat or rain or storm. There was hardly anything that she would say to anyone. She would attend the *Aarti*, sit down in silent contemplation, keep looking at her *Bappa* longingly, and sometimes keep smiling at him as if she was having a one-on-one conversation with Him. People around her never disturbed her. They knew her. They gave her way, allowing her to complete her meditation looking at *Bappa*, sitting right in front of the powerful idol. The unshed tear at the corner of her eye never flowed out. Every Tuesday, she was joined by her daughter, Sneha. That was when everyone heard her melodious voice. She spoke lovingly to the priest and offered a pack of *modaks* to her favourite *Ganesha.*

Ranjani had instilled values in her children right from the beginning. Her daughter, Sneha was now in her final year of engineering. It used to be a long journey, changing two local trains in the process. She had a first-class pass for her ease, especially during the peak hours. And wasn't she a replica of her mother in terms of punctuality? Exactly at 7.30 pm on Tuesdays, she would come to the Ganesha temple close to the station premises. In fact, most of the student fraternity would gather in the temple premises on Tuesdays. You could find most of the board exams giving kids of class XII or graduation courses offer their prostrations to this Lord of examinations. The Mulund East station *wala* Ganesha was known as exam Ganapati. All those who prayed here on Tuesdays were sure to succeed with flying colours. Sneha attended extra classes on Tuesdays and Thursdays. Exactly at 7.30 pm on Tuesdays, she used to walk into the temple, offer her prostrations to the Lord and then the duo of mother and daughter, slowly made their way back home around 8.00 pm, with Sneha rattling off about her friends and her college.

This week had been no different. It was Thursday, the 13th of March 2003. Sneha had accompanied her mom back home from the temple on 11th March, Tuesday. But approaching in the next few days were an important set of vivas and later campus placements also! No harm in visiting *Bappa* again and bribing him with a few *modaks* on coming Tuesday, if things worked out well. She told *Aai* that she would be taking the 7.45 pm fast local to Mulund and would join her at the temple today from where they could go home together.

7.45 pm… which means that Sneha would be in the temple by 7.46 pm. By 8.00 pm, slowly, they would be making their way home. She just had to make some rotis. Today she had made okra, which was Sneha's favourite and also *shrikhand*, which was Harish's favourite dish. She just had to go home and offer it to *Sai Baba* for His evening dinner *prasad* before serving it to all the family members. Thursday evenings always had a sweet that she offered to her Guru, Sai. In fact, her husband, Prakash had started looking out for Thursdays. What joy Ranjani derived by offering the sweet to *Sai Baba*! Her face used to be, as told by Prakash, very radiant during such times, the silence speaking volumes of the deep conversation that she was having with her Lord.

That evening, most people who had visited the temple for the Aarti purpose had already left. There were hardly a handful of people left in the temple. Ranjani was sitting in front of the idol, looking at Him compassionately, when loud noises could be heard, there was a huge commotion outside and people started running helter-skelter. Suddenly alerted, the few people who were there in the temple, started looking at each other. One known devotee came running into the temple and shouted, 'There has been a major bomb blast in the first-class ladies' compartment in the 7:45 pm local, right here at Mulund railway station. All of you please stay back, don't go out anywhere for a little while. This seems to be like a terrorist attack. Police have come, the area will soon be cordoned off.'

The priest and a few others present there, looked at Ranjani, who had unknowingly screamed and looked shocked. The tears had escaped her eyes now. 'My daughter Sneha said she would come here by train. She travels by the first-class ladies' compartment.' A visibly shocked priest could also say nothing. He slowly came to her, and so did the few others who were present there. 'At least a dozen people have died and lots many have been injured,' continued the devotee. 'It was a powerful blast. The whole compartment was in shambles. I was able to see it from the corner of this temple compound.'

Ranjani recovered and tried to move so as to peep from the same corner of the compound, but the priest stopped her. He led her back to the idol and made her sit down again, and slowly offered her a glass of water. '*Bappa* will take care,' he said. 'Maybe your child did not take this train,' he thoughtfully said. 'No, that is not possible, my children are never late, especially for trains, until and unless there is some emergency. Punctuality is one virtue that they are endowed with. My Harish, exactly ten years ago, wanted to share his Biology journal with his friend who had been absent. He had been doing very well and was all set to take up the pre-medical examination—PMT exam that summer. Don't you think he would have made such a fine doctor, one of the best neurosurgeons by now? His friend had been sick and had missed a few notes. Instead of him coming all the way to our home here in Mulund, Harish offered to meet him close to that very famous hotel, near his house. He took his Bio journal and his assignment notebook along with him. The bomb squad found my son's journal, with the beautiful diagrams of the human heart and the brain, a little bit burnt out, thrown far away by the impact of the powerful blast that day. He had been punctual, waiting for his friend, who had yet to reach the venue... No *pujari ji*, my children are never late. And I am being punished in this manner for teaching them such good values.'

The lady had finally broken her silence on this subject. It took her a decade, precise to the date. 12th March 1993, evening. Harish's body never found its way back home to his waiting parents. Today 13th March 2003—What would be the outcome? 'Are you asking me to go through all this once again Deva? Is my Harish not sufficient that you have given me a trying time again? Have you taken Sneha too now?' she tearfully asked the Lord.

As news reached far and wide across the city in the next hour, Ranjani sat down in the temple, in front of her *Ganaraj*, having wiped off her tears, sharing an unspoken conversation with him through her eyes. Eyes which were pleading with Him, eyes which suddenly were clouded in a few seconds, but quickly blinked away, eyes which spoke of faith, and eyes which spoke of acceptance to whatever awaited her. 'This time, at least let me have a last look at my child if you have taken her away. Last time, I didn't even get to see my son,' she told *Bappa*, before deciding to leave for home. The priest offered to walk the distance with her. He had been a witness to what this brave mother had undergone in the past decade, and in spite of which her faith in the Almighty had never even once been diminished or faltered. In spite of everything, every single day brought her back to the temple, to her *Bappa*. Not once did she complain, not once did she show her tears.

They reached home in a matter of ten more minutes. An equally shocked Prakash opened the door. They said nothing to each other, she went about with her task of making *rotis* and offering it with the other dishes to the Lord. *Pujari ji* and Prakash sat in the living room and switched on the TV. There were a few gory scenes of the compartment and of Mulund station. *Pujari ji* stood up to take leave of their family. It was precisely at that moment that the doorbell rang. Maybe, it was the police, maybe it was someone with information about Sneha. On the second ring, *pujari ji* went in and opened the door. Stood there half smiling, half crying, half scared Sneha. Sneha, in one piece, very much alive. She came in, into the warm embrace of her *Baba*. Her *Aai* came out, saw her, took a few deep breaths, and moved back to her kitchen, where there was a small *devghar*, her temple, where her *Ganesha* resided, where her Sai resided. She joined her hands in gratitude to these wonder superhumans, without whom this miracle wasn't possible.

Sneha looked at *Aai*, came to her, hugged her tightly and related what had happened. She was crossing the road at Andheri station when her eyes fell on a little boy who was also trying to cross it. He had no adult beside him to help. She went close to him, and held his hand, helping him across. The road was a busy one, and it took time for her, more than what it generally took to cross it. When he smiled back at her, she lingered for a moment more and asked him his name. His reply was 'Harish.' On hearing his name, she somehow felt connected and spent a few more minutes with him. By the time she got on to the station, she was shocked by the elapsed time. She was late, and she missed her local train. The next one was due only after 12 minutes. As Sneha reminded herself again and again that she meant to do good for the child, she now knew that she would be late at Dadar station as well, and then she would miss the 7.45 pm fast local to Mulund. Alas! Poor lady, *Aai* would be waiting for her. She finally took a slow local train that would have a halt at Mulund around 8.01 pm. The rest of the story was known to everyone.

As Ranjani slowly told a silent prayer of gratitude for the wellbeing of this unknown child that Sneha met on the street this day, because of whom she got late, Sneha looked at the smiling face of her Harish Dada's garlanded photograph, which seemed to say, 'Today, I have not backed away from my responsibility, I made sure that you got late because of my namesake, and hence the sequence of events of missing the train.' Being late at such times proves to be a boon in disguise. A happy family slowly bowed down in gratitude to *Bappa* and *Sai Baba* and thanked Them for keeping all of them hale and healthy.

A Broken Tale

Gairik Misra

Sadness is what now, carries my heart,

Within the joyous sorrows of the past.

As for now, we depart,

To depart ourselves, be last,

But alas!

Over the bridge darkness lies,

A dance of thousand fireflies.

The world is forever round,

As my clock confound.

No longer can I reach the ground,

Never lost, never found.

Dark alley, river, grass,

Blue stained glass,

But alas!

Far Away Land

Avinash Sadaphule

I love my partner,

But he is toxic.

He takes me to faraway places,

Calling them exotic.

I despair about his behaviour,

Although he acts as my only saviour.

I share with him my all wants,

But he does not show me any response.

I long for my home

When I am home alone.

To the love of my parents,

I long to go away from this tyrant.

Oh! The dreams I had,

If I leave all this, they will call me mad.

I don't care anymore,

My heart is not here anymore.

I feel so hopeless,

Now I am nothing but clueless.

I stay in a palace,

Everyone believes I am still a princess.

Alas! I don't want a palace,

In this wonderland, I don't want to be Alice.

I just want a dome,

That I can truly call my home.

I don't lose hope,

I never say nope.

A day will come soon

When I will be back home and over the moon.

My life is not null,

I believe there is light at the end of the tunnel.

Nothing else can go wrong

When I rise and be so strong.

I will thrive

And survive,

To go back to my loved ones, hand in hand,

From this faraway land…

From this far away land…

Agonising Ages

Anushka Rathi

It's been ages since you tucked my hair,

It's been ages since I have felt pretty.

Of tales, mysteries, hymns and tunes,

Feelings ineffable and beauties inexpressible.

I read your letters on a gloomy day, lazy afternoons,

I want to fall in so deep,

but I realise ponds are many, and oceans are only five.

In the end, it is not you, but myself, I despise.

It's scary how people scare me nowadays,

The smiles that seemed friendly yesterday.

Now catch me off guard, my feelings on the bay,

Of sadness, anger that can mature only from love,

But love turns ugly, fondness turns filthy,

Apprehension takes over your veins and brain.

Pain seeps in through your heart and bleeds

Till you are drowning in its blues,

That's when it hits you,

He wasn't my home; he was a house.

Resiliencia—Spirit of Mumbai!

Smruti Tilak

'Gooooood Morning Mumbai!' greeted RJ Malini, as she went live on her FM show.

Two decades back for many Mumbaikars, this is how the day began. When mobile phones were not smart but intelligent enough to outdate the Walkman. The inbuilt FM channels in the cell phones entertained the users.

'*Sakali Sakali jaataye tari kuthe?*' (Where are you headed early in the morning?) asked Malini in an inquisitive tone.

Jyoti Satam froze as she heard her favourite RJ.

Jyoti, a beautiful ambitious girl in her early twenties, was on platform number 1 of the Borivali station in Mumbai. She was heading towards the 7.14 am Churchgate fast local train. It was the same local train that she boarded every day to ensure she reached her office on time.

Malini's words echoed in her ears and a sense of fear gripped her. Where was she heading this morning, she questioned herself. 'To work, of course,' replied her inner voice.

But why? Today was not a regular morning, it was the 12th of July 2006.

Less than 24 hours back, the local trains, known as Mumbai's lifeline, were paralysed. Mumbai's *dhadkan* or heartbeat, the local trains were subjected to a series of bomb blasts by some terrorist outfits. The fateful evening was disastrous. The loss was immeasurable.

Jyoti's wandering mind teleported her to the second-class general compartment which she had boarded with her friend, Sourabh. The evening local from Lower Parel was fixed, the compartment was fixed and so were their train pals. Train pals were a group of people who may not be known by name but become an integral part of our travelogue as they board the same train each day.

As the train crossed Mahim, Sourabh got a call. It was his colleague. There was a major client escalation, and they were asked to report back to work immediately. This fumed Sourabh.

Both Jyoti and Sourabh worked together in an esteemed Call Centre at Phoenix Mall, Lower Parel. The BPO sector was a new boom where clients were revered as God. Everything was done to please the divine and client satisfaction was the ultimate target. Jyoti understood the gravity of the situation and non-adherence meant getting a pink slip. She convinced Sourabh to head back to work. After initial reluctance, he agreed, and both alighted the train at Andheri.

Sourabh was irritated, and annoyed as he walked to the other side of the platform to catch a Southbound train. It was then that the chaos began.

The news was spared like a forest fire. Frantically calls were made by all, and messaging services collapsed. Had they heard it correctly?

A bomb had exploded in a train as it approached Jogeshwari station, the station after Andheri. The explosion was in the very compartment they had exited a few minutes back.

Trembling, shaking, with fear in their eyes, breathing rapidly, sweating, they froze. The call from their colleague had saved them. Had they not alighted the train, fate would have taken another turn.

They felt a shrill in their spine.

In the next few minutes, the Western Railway line collapsed. There were a series of blasts that scared the city. Each Mumbaikar prayed for the safety of their loved ones.

Jyoti and Sourabh had a miraculous escape but not all were lucky. Few lost their lives. The city wept in the deep dark night. The night seemed the longest as if there would be no morning. The city of dreams had its worst nightmare.

It was around midnight, and Jyoti reached home, yet to recover from the shock. The terrorist that killed many with their evil plans must have felt elated that night. Little did they know, they can never kill the spirit of Mumbai.

The morning of July 12 was eerie but picked up the pace. True Mumbaikar is resilient. He is a fighter and will rise back after a storm like a rising Sun.

Jyoti, too, was a Mumbai girl and was determined not to get scared of these terror attacks and report to work the next day.

She hoped justice would soon prevail and the masterminds behind such heinous crimes would be punished. She said a silent prayer for the many citizens who lost their lives, adjusted her earphone and heard RJ Malini's voice, 'Stay tuned for our next song, *Jaara Haatke, Jaara Bachke, Yeh hai Bombay meri Jaan!*'

Be Yourself

Mallika Chandrasekhar

Truly,

Eventually, all other personas,

Will peel away.

Fragile egos,

False exteriors,

Projected attributes,

And conditioned notions,

Will be stripped from you.

Like the dried leaves of a tree,

Be yourself.

However, you are,

Vulnerable,

Fearful,

Loveable,

Gullible.

You can choose to,

Be what others want you to be.

Indeed, you do,

You behave, talk and think,

What others want to talk and think,

For being accepted,

For being popular,

But then, too many become you,

And you become less you.

Just a collectable,

Of public impressions,

And judgments.

At the end of a work day,

You wonder at the void,

The vacant spot in place of your heart,

You brush it off as fatigue.

But actually, it's oblique,

Reflections, disaffections,

You gain neither rest nor peace,

For you left yourself,

The truest purest part of you,

Somewhere behind,

In the mighty crowd,

Of friends, family, and strangers.

Be yourself,

For you came with it,

Your SELF.

You will also leave with it.

You can surrender to a Higher Self,

In fact, you must.

You can share yourself,

Indeed, you should.

But never leave being yourself,

Not parts or dissected fragments,

But the whole of you,

Authentic,

Imperfect,

Be yourself.

It's the best self,

For you.

Second Chances

Mallika Chandrasekhar

A broken dream,

Or a heart.

A dead relationship

Or a loved one lost.

A missing feeling,

Or a possibility gone naughty.

A way of being misled,

Or a memory wiped out.

First-time losses

Are very hard.

First-time disasters and disappointments

Are the most painful and tragic.

But they don't have to be that,

Not always.

Because every one of us,

Gets one of these,

SECOND CHANCES.

Take them,

More reverentially,

More gratefully.

Then the first,

Second Chances mean,

You deserve it, so you got it.

The Realisation

Dimple Makkhija

The break from you moved mountains,

It really shook a part of me.

Broken, shattered and lost in my own world,

Led to the birth of an unworthy me.

The days passed, the months passed,

But there was something changing.

However wounded it seemed,

There was still a will to stand all over again.

Beginning to love every moment of my being,

A realisation of hope.

Was that inner voice trying to tell me,

How unfaithful I had been!

Giving others a priority over myself,

What a grave mistake I had committed.

Never mind a revolution had occurred,

Making the life I ever dreamt.

Learning unlearning,

The nitty gritty transformed.

Stagnancy to movement,

Finally, the plant finally began to flower.

The Beauty of Wrinkles

Sumakalyani Ganti

Two years of homeschooling! Complete two years. Like many of his friends, Raja never knew how two years passed. In relief initially, with fright and fear when the second wave of Covid-19 was at its peak, totally broken down at times, in amazement at times, in thankfulness as well, but somehow two years got over for everyone at home. Raja would now come to third grade. His first and second grades had been online. He had gone to the regular school during his pre-school and kindergarten days, which means he never knew school. His neighbour, Bittu *bhaiyya* would start his fifth grade now. But he had at least gone to school! Raja was about to start his real school when Covid took over the whole world, and everything had to close down. Slowly they found means to open educational institutions and classes started in online mode.

What had initially started as a fun thing, slowly became boring and also a learning experience, by the end of two years. Oh, what fun were the initial days. The teachers used to take a roll count, and by that time some children used to have a power cut. The teacher used to say, 'Switch on your videos.' Then again, she would ask if everyone got ready, had a bath, had eaten breakfast etc., slowly all of them who were in first grade used to speak the truth. Teachers used to tell them how it was important for them to be ready just like how they would come to school. Many kids did not understand the importance of these things. Raja now remembered how his class teacher used to have these lines on her forehead when she used to explain to them again and again about these things. The same lines as those which Mummy used to have daily these days—not these days, but since the past six months. Maybe the teacher had also been sad, that's what mummy said when she first saw his class and then told him. Since that day, he tried his best not to make the teacher sad. But now Mummy was sad, he could see those lines often, especially more since his daddy said bye to them from the hospital itself during the second wave. After that everything was a haze.

Now that school had started again, he found that he did not like lines anymore. Creases—that's what someone had joked about. It had been a week since third grade had started, and he really was looking forward to wearing his uniform, saying bye to mummy, going to real school and coming back home for his food, not just moving from room to room. Now that Daddy wasn't there, he used to see how mummy used to work outside as well as at home. Old granny just used to sit outside on the balcony quietly the whole day, remembering her son. He did not want to trouble anyone more and get more of those sad lines on their foreheads. He was big enough! He would try to solve things by himself. But if he did not tell what was bothering him, would those lines come on his forehead too? He went and looked at himself in the mirror—yes, yes, those lines were there! His sadness could be seen on those lines on his forehead. Now, now, can't talk about all these to either mummy or *Dadi.*

Since Daddy had gone away, they hadn't purchased any new clothes. He had yearned so much for a neat and new school uniform and to be a shining star in his class. But, last week, Bittu's mother came and handed over a set of old clothes that Bittu *bhaiyya* was done with. In it were two sets of uniforms as well. They were all used clothes, but he was trying to adjust. They did not have much money. Mummy never told him, but he did understand. After the whole day at school, when he came home, he threw away his clothes in the laundry basket and Mummy would wash them. Since there were two sets, he was using each of them on alternate days. But when he wore them for school the next day, straight from the clothesline, they were full of lines, just like those sad lines.... what were they called? Some kids in his class had started making fun of him, they said, 'Raja, you have so many of those lines.... wrinks.... yes, wrinkles on your clothes.' He did not like it. Daddy always used to go to the office in neat and beautiful clothes. He used to give his ironing clothes for ironing to the watchman downstairs. But since the advent of covid, the watchman uncle had stopped this work. He would not touch anyone's things—especially from their house, since there had been a covid death in the family.

Maybe he could wash his uniform by himself and dry it on the line, and then no lines would come. The next day, much to the questioning look of Dadi and mummy, Raja tried to wash his clothes. After a few minutes, he realised that he was in a disastrous position. He confided in mummy a little bit, that he was trying to help with clothes. Mummy smiled. And you know what? The lines on her forehead became less! Sad Lines on your forehead become less when smiling curves appear on your face! He went and checked for himself in the mirror, but no! His lines were still there, which meant that if you smile from the heart, only then those forehead lines would go off. If you smile superficially, then the lines remain.

So, washing by himself would not work. Well, he would take the clothes off the lines by himself and fold them neatly. Maybe then he would have less of creases and wrinkles. So, for the next few days, he tried but the uniform ended up more wrinkled than before. After a few days of unsuccessful struggle, he knew it wasn't worth it. He came back to the mirror and looked at himself. Looks like he got one more line on his forehead when he went and pushed his nose onto the mirror and tried to peer into his image. Yes, today three kids laughed at him, because they felt his uniform was not so new, nor was it ironed. He couldn't be a shiny star.

He went down to the watchman of the building and asked him if he could iron his uniform. The watchman said, 'Rs. 8 per cloth, so Rs. 16 per set of uniform.' Well, that was too much. His mom was working so hard, he could not waste money like this.

Now, what to do? Pondering over this, he sat down in the living room. Mummy had gone to the shop today to buy a few things. It had been so long since she had gone shopping. Since Daddy had passed away, she hadn't gone out much. The initial few months were just about isolation, no one could visit them, and neither could they go out. Then mummy had fallen sick, and there was no one to care for them, mainly because of the isolation. Thankfully, mummy had recovered enough. Now that those times had passed away, and mummy had gotten a job and his school had started, they were stitching up their life again. Trivial things like uniform and wrinkles did not matter so much, in the wake of what he had undergone the past few months. Kids laughing at him did not know all these, hence probably this reaction from them.

He somehow needed to manage his things, without troubling his mother. Now, it was time to be responsible and help his mother. Not bother her with these wrinkles on his clothes, else the wrinkles on her forehead would increase, forget about more wrinkles gathering on the wrinkled body of *Dadi*! He smiled.

Now he knew what to do. When mummy folded his clothes, he would take them and keep them under the bed. It would turn out to be as good as ironed ones. No wrinkles on his uniform anymore! He ran to the mirror and the creases on his forehead just reduced or rather disappeared!

Mummy walked in from her shopping, he smiled at her and ran to get her a glass of water. 'Now, why is my Raja all smiles today?' asked mummy. 'And I purchased something that would be useful for both you and me,' said Mom after drinking water. Raja looked at mummy, as she removed something from the shopping bag. It was an iron.

She looked so sweetly at him, took him into her arms, made him sit on her lap and said that she had been noticing his strife and struggle the whole week. But she was so proud of him! He was such a responsible child; not once did he ask her for help. Now that they had their own iron, they could straighten off all the wrinkles. 'Mummy, also those wrinkles on your forehead,' asked Raja innocently. 'Yes, *beta*, those too, with a smiling curve of your face,' beamed a smiling mother. A wrinkled *Dadi* also erased a few difficult lines on her forehead, seeing their smiles, and added on a few soothing wrinkles with her huge smile. With gratitude, and a silent prayer on her lips, for whatever still sustained in spite of the pandemic, mummy decided to do away with a few wrinkles on her forehead too.

Wake Up

Carol Mitra

There is sweat in my eyes,

On my palms and in my hair,

Making me cry from every pore.

The sky burning up, fevered air,

Hot torrid winds spreading disease.

The weather already quite dead,

Leaves crinkling under my feet,

I look up at the sky now turning brown.

It burns hot, my skin on fire,

And I can feel the earth's pain.

The insects are awfully noisy,

No sound of sweet birds,

Strange the sun is growing bigger and bigger,

How is it getting so hot?

I reach home now it smells of rot.

I put myself to bed and sleep,

Till I roll off my burning cot.

It's scorching hot! The smell keeps me bound,

I look out and see the whole city burning.

Screams swallowed by the ground,

It is inevitable, this destruction,

By design we are takers,

We have created endless mistakes.

This crazy man-made intervention,

The unforgiving blue sea rising,

Cool the Earth down degree by degree.

Education on conservation

Can eradicate this human catastrophe,

Using our resources responsibly.

Wake up! The Earth is breathtaking,

Living and breathing for you and me!

The Stranger

Kavita Singh

I have sown a seed in the grasses,

In the longing of my own tree.

Waited for days and months and then moved on to live,

My heart was full of love and so I found one to shower at.

The world started to seem to be a better and happier place,

It was like a smile has made my face its all-time home.

But then clouds above my head moved away and unveiled the truth,

My heart was broken, and my eyes were full of tears.

I lay down on the floor open-handed to feel some touch,

Thinking that all the way and all the years I was wrong,

There were everywhere pain and stain,

It was not easy to shed tears about which no one was aware.

Then I found a doom of dense leaves, underneath which I cried and screamed,

And found myself hugged by a stranger as if someone own.

And realised the next moment it was the same tree once which I have sown.

The Tomorrow

Kavita Singh

If it was summer, when someone has left,

Scars on your heart,

You may hate then, the scorching heat,

And a shiny long day,

That has turned your green grass into hay.

May the pleasant monsoon, fail to put off the fire, burning inside
you,

Tears keep falling secretly, hiding behind the incessant rain,

But the time will come with a magic wand,

To dry your eyes to show how beautiful life is.

A cool breeze blowing in the dusk and dawn,

Rustling of leaves and birds chirping in the lawn,

Alluding the new season with dews and drops,

Farms flaunting wheat, barley and winter crops.

Take a deep breath and come out from your pain,

Learn to live with your loss and see what you can gain,

It will be surely hard to walk with a heavy heart along the slope,

But then only tomorrow will be abreast with rise and hope.

The Multiverse Needs a Mother

Deepika Chalke

Have you ever felt the need to understand someone's heart? Because you want to understand what kind of heart creates pain and suffering rather than love and beauty? I am talking about the heart of the multiverse. It's a living, breathing thing that countless scientists across universes have tried to find and understand. Their reasons are different from mine. They want to learn the secrets of time travel, and immortality, and worse: they want to clone the heart of the multiverse. They say their scientific endeavours are driven by curiosity and will benefit all universes. I don't care what they say—they are a bunch of cookie monsters, and they see the heart of the multiverse as a jar of cookies to gobble and satisfy their unending carnal, selfish impulses.

The way the scientists are approaching this problem is different from the way I am tackling it. They are driven by their head and rationality; I am driven by a broken heart and pain.

Their system has two levels: a heart finder that will scan the multiverse for its heart and once found, a heart reader will be deployed at the specific coordinates to read it. The heart of the multiverse is where all universes connect, a dead end, a singularity, a mystery.

I am only going to build a heart reader, not a heart finder. Why? If

I can build a heart reader that has the exact same frequencies as the heart of the multiverse, my device will be able to download information from the heart of the multiverse right here in my lab in a few seconds. Simple, right? Not really.

I have made thousands of heart readers. They have all failed.

What kind of frequencies does the heart of the multiverse carry?

Infinite power, mystery, magic, complex life, death, infinite wisdom, infinite light, infinite dark, infinite dreams, infinite healing, infinite compassion?

None of these frequencies in any permutation and combination worked.

One night, reeling from the worst bout of pain and anger I have ever had to endure, I finally created a heart reader that began receiving messages from the heart of the multiverse.

I almost spilt scalding hot coffee over my body when I heard the first message. Can you guess what it said?

'You are in pain. I am in pain. You feel broken. I feel broken. You feel alone. I feel alone. You know what that means, right?'

That was the message. My first thought was that someone's hacked into the heart of the multiverse and is fooling with me.

'Excuse me? Stop wasting my heart reader's bandwidth. Who are you? Identify yourself, thief! How did you gain control of the heart of the multiverse? And why are you sending childish messages my way?' That's the message my heart reader and I passed on to the impostor pretending to be the heart of the multiverse.

'Read me the frequencies of your heart reader.' The hacker responded.

'No way, punk.' I refused.

'Pain. That's it. That's your heart reader's frequency because that's your heart's dominant frequency. And that's my frequency.'

'Shut up. Don't make me build a heart destroyer. I swear I will do it if you say another word.' I snapped in anger, feeling slightly light-headed.

'That's not all. Our frequency of pain is so eerily alike that we are inextricably interconnected. You are an orphan. I am an orphan; we both have no knowledge or memory of warmth and love.'

I dropped the mug; I didn't care that I spilled coffee all over me. The only thing that mattered was shutting the damn heart reader. I was shaking and in a fit of childish anger, I threw the heart reader onto the floor. It looked like a mangled corpse and for a second, I felt like a murderer. But then I was relieved. No more demented, soul-tormenting messages from the scary, heartless heart of the multiverse.

'You didn't have to destroy that poor thing. Like I was saying—we are connected; we are family. We will forever be able to hear each other, understand each other.'

I was spooked beyond my wits. The damn heart was speaking to me without any heart reader.

'I am not looking for a family. You are not my family. I just wanted to understand what kind of heart creates pain and suffering. I have my answer.'

'Tell me—what's the answer?' The heartless heart of the multiverse kept yapping.

'A heart that is in pain and suffering creates pain and suffering. How stupid of me to have built a heart reader to answer such a simple question. Even an idiot could have answered it.'

'You are not stupid. And you know the solution to our misery, right?'

'Build a heart destroyer to destroy your heart,' I responded, feeling slightly exhausted, engaging in a dead-end conversation.

'You don't mean that. If my heart is destroyed, universes across the cosmos will lose their hearts and life everywhere will cease to exist.'

'Build you a family! That's it. What kind of family do you want?

Once you have a family, your heart's pain will be healed. And a healed heart will create love and beauty. And everyone everywhere will know love and beauty and not pain and suffering.' I had never been so happy; I had never felt so brilliant.

'You. I want you as my family.' The heart of the multiverse said gently.

I had trouble breathing.

'That sounds like an ominous death sentence. No way. The sound of it makes me uncomfortable. Stop saying creepy things, please.'

'Take it or leave it. That is the deal!' The heart responded in a kind but firm tone.

'Deal? I am not here to make any deals with you. Just please leave me alone.'

'No.'

'Stop acting like a six-year-old. I am not your mother.' I replied, feeling tired, flabbergasted, and amused at how childlike the heart of the multiverse was.

'Mother! Mother! You can be my mother. Yes, you would make a wonderful mother.'

'Excuse me? You are infinitely older than me; if anything, you should be my mother.'

'We can take turns being a mother. But first, it's your turn.'

'What do I know about being a mother? I have never had a mother.'

'You were born to be a mother. As per my wisdom computer, a mother is someone who wants to know the heart of her child; so, she can give the child love and warmth and eliminate all pain and suffering. Isn't that the purpose with which you set out to find my heart?'

'No. I just wanted to understand your heart because I was curious and in pain. I wasn't looking to play a healer or a mother. I just could not understand why the most powerful force to ever exist was creating pain instead of creating love.'

'To want to understand why someone's heart is in pain without expecting anything in return is an act of love.' The multiverse responded.

'Enough of these cheesy, crappy lines, please! Fine. I will be your mother. As your mother, I forbid you from uttering such sentimental hogwash. Though I am curious, is your heart feeling warmth and love right now? Are you...are you free of your pain?'

'Yes, mother. Are you free of your pain?'

'Oddly, I feel free from a meaningless, heartless destiny for the first time ever. I feel like I am needed, like I have a purpose, like I am loved and free to love, not doomed; not cursed.'

And that was the end of a long, solo walk that two souls had endured until mystery and magic weaved their paths together into a happy ending.

I Accept No Defeat

Vishakha Naware

With a smile plastered on my face,

I face this oblivious world,

Beneath the façade of my dimpled cheeks,

Is a bleeding heart,

Broken into a million pieces,

By none other than you.

I loved you more than anything,

In this world full of beauty,

Loving you was my favourite duty,

Suddenly one day the clouds turned black,

And I sat waiting for you near the windowsill,

While everything I wished for went downhill.

While life has to go on like clockwork,

I can't help but think of it backwards,

To the time when we were together,

When sunset felt more beautiful with you,

I know, you have gone away, far away.

But I will not accept defeat,

Winning you back is no mean feat.

But I will win you back,

With all my love,

My resolve will not crack.

Till I get you back,

This time I'll not dove,

No one can stop me; I accept no defeat!

You are Complete

Vishakha Naware

Have you ever felt so,

As if your life is about to fall apart?

Love and life have abandoned you,

Faith and hope have waved goodbye?

Have you ever felt so,

All the happiness that was once your friend,

Left you with a baggage of memories,

Far away, never to be found again?

Have you ever felt so,

Amazement and wonder have renounced you,

Leaving you in a deep void,

Filling you with disappointment and contempt?

Have you felt so,

As if you are half the person you ever were,

Limited functioning, on autopilot,

Fed up with everything that's around you?

Have you ever felt so,

A lingering feeling of being incomplete?

Let it feel that way,

For sometimes you need to feel that way.

Come on now,

Off you go,

Meander no more,

Pardon yourself,

Let it go,

Every day is a new beginning,

Train yourself to believe in you,

Everything will be fine!

Half no more, you are complete, when you are you!

Light on The Other Side

Adwaith Jayan

A sorrowful year for many,
And a sunny one for a few,
Many did cry and many did die.

Honey, I know it's dark outside,
But there's light on the other side,
When will we reach there?
I don't know, but I can swear,
That we will be there.

But while we're here,
All that's left for you and me is
Me and you.

I see the dark clouds outside,
But I know arcs of colour follow,
Stay with me, will you?
Honey, we don't need to hide.

Many did cry and many did die,

Let's not forget that,

When we reach the other side!

The Known Alphabet of Life

Sumakalyani Ganti

It is all a play of letters—standing lines, sleeping lines, slanting lines and curves. Letters would make words, words would make sentences, sentences would make paragraphs, paragraphs would make chapters, chapters would make books, and these books enhance you. Shilpa loved reading books, books that were filled with knowledge, books full of fun, facts, opinions, space, encyclopaedias, and what not. Knowledge empowers you; books make your life. Nothing feels better than taking a book in hand, sitting without anyone disturbing you and not knowing how time flies by! Shilpa loved reading, she absolutely loved books. And these same books, chapters, paragraphs, sentences, alphabet, letters, lines and curves would torture her innocent, lovely son in the future!

Is this what the doctor was saying? Ashu was still too little and was playing with small things, blocks and balls, a car and a truck! She looked at him endearingly. He was indeed the most beautiful, adorable child that she had ever seen. Chubby, fair-skinned with large eyes. He was so normal, just like every other child. In fact, he was the best! Just then he looked up at her, smiled broadly and showed her the big new car that he was holding in his hand. Her precious son, her precious baby. She smiled back. A bike screeched outside. '*Ammmmma*,' he screamed, having dropped the car, and holding his ears with both his palms.

Dr Kamath was kind-hearted. Every parent who came to him felt that their child was absolutely normal, with probably just a little bit of slight behavioural change. It was always a tough job for him to observe these children over a period of a few days, check their patterns and draw a conclusion. It was always difficult for him to break news to them that their child had an abnormal element to their behaviour.

Ashutosh was near his mom, with this almost nice uncle. The last few days *Amma* was getting him here, and this uncle wasn't really trying to get close to him. There weren't many noises here. At home, people kept moving—here and there, from room to room. Ashu, Ashu, Ashu! He couldn't bear to hear everyone constantly calling out. Probably that was his name. When Amma called him, he always looked at her and said, '*Aaanh?*' When anyone else called him, he never even felt like looking at them. They kept calling again and again, it was so frustrating!

The other people—they were so noisy. They spoke to each other, to him, to the outsiders, who kept ringing that irritating doorbell in some unfathomable language that he could not decipher, and then they kept looking at him, was he also supposed to reply? He did, but they wouldn't understand. He tried to avoid them; he was always on the lookout for *Amma*. Only she would not keep the chatter going. She would simply come near him, speak softly, and make action with her hand and eye movements. She would soothe him with her touch.

Then came those sudden, terrible, frightening, scary sounds, if he ventured out into the balcony. They were cars, trucks, autos, buses, very noisy things. Daddy held him at those times. Sometimes, they were so irritating that he screamed at them, asking them to stop. He screamed at those people who disturbed him with their doorbell sounds. And he screamed at those people who constantly kept moving in the house. He asked them to stop! But everyone kept looking strangely at him as if something was wrong in the manner in which he asked them to stop. How he wished *Amma* would just take him to some serene place, where only calmness prevailed, away from these noises, away from these disturbing people, away from these irritating sounds! Yes, Daddy was also good. He picked him up, gave him a broad smile and spoke softly to him. Grandparents were also good, they spoke gently, but not those other relatives who constantly used to come home. So many people used to come, and they used to talk in loud voices, used to keep laughing, used to keep moving around him.

Yes, Ashutosh liked only two people—*Amma* and Daddy. The rest of them seemed like intruders. And yes, he preferred silence, and he preferred solitude. He could then see the beauty of things around him and speak to the person who created them too. He would actually come and talk to him every day, not in the gibberish language that these people spoke, but in silence.

He told *Amma* that he was meeting this person every day, and was talking to Him, they spoke in silence, so that no one else was distributed. Seems even *Amma* did not understand. Ashu was speaking in words and sentences, but Amma was the only word he knew. How much ever Amma tried to tell him other words, this remained his favourite. He spoke only one word. And that word was "*Amma*". As the bike screeched outside, the noise triggered off something in him. That bike fellow was about to crush him. He tightly shut his eyes, closed his ears with both his hands, and asked him to *stoooooop*! In the one word known to him.

'*Ammmmmmma!*'

Amma came running to him and held him. Slowly Ashutosh calmed down and started playing with his car again. *Amma* managed to get the bike fellow away from him. 'There was so much calmness here since he had been coming for the past few days. Where did this terrible bike sound come from today?' he wondered.

He saw the almost, nice uncle in the white coat, and the almost nice aunty in her white dress, all of them looking out from the window. Dr

Kamath saw the effect of this sound on this three-year-old child, Ashutosh. This centre was in a quiet place amidst nature, far away, on the outskirts of the city. Generally, never disturbed by such sounds. Looks like the bike had some trouble and had suddenly halted with a screeching sound. He carefully observed the impact it had on Ashutosh. The way his mother Shilpa held him and soothed him had truly reassured him.

As *Amma* started speaking with the doctor in the strange language again, Ashu got back to silently playing with the toys around him. 'As I was telling you, Shilpa and Rajesh, it's all a play of letters. The brain would understand only the patterns that it is able to fathom and can recognise only certain signals, these signals are not reaching the other parts of the body, immediately, because of sensory delays. He has a developmental disorder that impairs his ability to communicate and interact. When did you last notice that something could have been wrong with Ashu?'

Shilpa was in tears. Rajesh and Shilpa had been getting their three-year-old son here, to Dr Kamath for the past week. She had sought the help of a speech therapist after their family doctor noticed that his milestones were not very apt. The speech therapist in turn had directed them to Dr Kamath, who was an expert in developmental issues. There had been discussions the past few months, in their house and taunts from relatives, regarding Ashutosh. 'Kids in our house would have been singing songs by now. All he says is *Amma*!! He keeps picking up only one single book, reads the same page again and again, picks up the blocks in the wrong manner, he is unable to put even simple puzzles together.' Shilpa was getting tired of these constant comparisons and taunts.

'By the time he was two years old, I noticed that Ashu was not able to speak much except for *Amma*, he responded only to me, he was scared of sounds, of crowds, of laughter, of movements around him. We tried to celebrate his birthday, but he was only crying the whole time. He used to get irritated with anyone around him. He tried to communicate, but it never reached us. No one understood what he was saying, so it was very frustrating for him. We observed him for a few months, and he seemed to be happier with just us around him. If any relative joined us, or if we took him to any park, mall or amusement centre, he would get very disturbed. We thought we needed to consult a doctor only after that.'

'He has been very normal since birth, it's only now in the past few months that we felt something was wrong. I'm sure we can work on it and bring him to normalcy.'

Dr Kamath heard her. Mothers are very special angels created by God. They have inherent strength and unconditional faith and hope. But they also are the most vulnerable. He looked at Shilpa and Rajesh. They were filled with questions and hope.

Breaking out this truth was one of the most difficult tasks for Dr Kamath. Especially in these cases which would have a lifelong impact and disrupt life. He looked at Ashutosh, the child looked so very normal, so very adorable. But no, he could not go closer to the child or touch him. Such children get scared very easily and this impression sticks with them. He only observed him from a distance the past few days. He did not want to waste any more time and effort of this family. The sooner they know the truth the better.

'Does he have a condition called ADHD?' asked Rajesh. He had a friend whose child suffered from ADHD. He had trouble focusing, but not communicating. In fact, that child spoke non-stop, went from person to person, looked at what everyone was doing, and kept speaking to everyone. He was hyperactive, so could not focus. His Ashutosh wasn't like that. 'Or is it dyslexia? That is also to do with trouble with letters, alphabets, numbers, and mirror images. But here too, the child speaks and mingles with people.'

'No, not these both. Certainly, both are to do with behavioural disorders, but Ashutosh has a neurodevelopmental disorder, called autism spectrum disorder (ASD) or Autism. Early diagnosis is very prominent here. Since you have brought your child here at the correct time, you first need to understand a few things. You need to be strong so that you do not get your fears or irritation onto him. First and foremost, your child is always, and will always be normal to you, but others may not feel that way. Acceptance is varying. Trying to get him into mainstream studies or activities will only result in turbulence in his already frustrating life. But he has a beauty that no one can comprehend. He may not be able to do simple things like regular reading or studies or games that other children do but end up being an expert in some other activities that he is fond of. Ashutosh might be an absolute genius in the future. At this stage, you need to go back home, compose yourself, do your research and be prepared to give your son a life that he needs and enjoys, not necessarily what others want him to become.'

'He might not be able to communicate with people that he is not comfortable with, and he might not be able to comprehend very small things like letters and numbers as well. These letters confuse him. These lines and curves cannot reach his brain. Someday, suddenly he might just like the way a slanting line or a sleeping line looks and decide that he likes this particular letter. Then he will go nonstop learning only that letter and things related to that repeatedly until he decides to move on to something new. If you send him to a regular school, you will only lose your child. As I said, acceptance is very low, though he might be accepted, he cannot immediately play with these letters and numbers. Cannot form words. Not everyone is patient enough to go out of the box and accommodate him.' Shilpa was sobbing.

That was when Ashu saw *Amma* crying. When he came to her, he remembered how *Amma* took care of him, when he was crying. He wiped her tears with his little fingers, gently said *Amma* and shook his head and moved his right index finger sideways. Then he gave her a hug, resting his head onto her bosom. No one in that room expected that kind of behaviour from Ashutosh. Rajesh was devoid of words, and so were Dr Kamath and the resident nurse. Shilpa was speechless! This was exactly how she used to calm him down when he started crying.

'See, this means that he remembers. Ashu's brain cells are able to retain your behaviour pattern. He feels your emotions too. He knows that something hurts you and you are crying, so he should comfort you. It's a matter of time, Shilpa. You can mould him. You can slowly teach him and reach out to people who are like-minded. Don't try to teach him letters or the alphabet or numbers. Do them in front of him. He will reciprocate it. It's time to get back to your basics in writing letters with the help of standing and sleeping lines. It's indeed a play of letters. When he sees you doing all these and enjoying the activities, he would start copying you.

But you need to give him space, only then he will flourish. If you get bogged down by the harsh taunts that others throw at you, you will never be able to make him independent. He might be gifted in other areas too, but he would need constant encouragement and initiative to explore things that he might start liking. There are many! You have to stand up for your child, Shilpa. All the best!'

Rajesh and Shilpa mumbled their thanks to Dr Kamath. They picked up their little Ashutosh in their arms and slowly made their way home. It was the time for making decisions.

Five years down the line, Dr Kamath was called as the chief guest at the annual day. He had agreed to it, on the condition that all the activities be performed right in front of him. They shouldn't have done it the previous week and just award the final prizes here. There were around 50 participating students of varying age groups. He knew most of them and their families. The teachers and the principal had already decided that every student needs to be rewarded, not for winning here, but for participating in the activities. Even if some student falls back and is unable to handle the sudden sounds or crowd, or throws a tantrum, it is ok. Trained teachers and volunteers would try to soothe them, and make sure that they do not miss any of the fun or appreciation, or that their family feels guilty about the wastage of time. He saw a beaming Ashutosh, now eight years old. He kept looking at the audience every few minutes. Once he located his mother Shilpa, he was at ease, all set to participate in his school's annual day activity.

Rajesh and Shilpa had gone back home that day, with little Ashutosh in their arms, saddened by the fact that their child was a special child, needed more care, more attention and had to be kept away from the prying eyes and ears of unwanted gossips and unsolicited advice. The next few months were very decisive. They did a lot of research on this disorder, and Shilpa tried to involve Ashu in small things like brushing his teeth and wearing clothes by himself. She kept encouraging him for every small thing that he did. Rajesh took up a job that needed very less travelling, and that involved more of a work-from-home model. They searched for like-minded individuals in the vicinity, with whom they could identify and with whom they could share the milestones of their child. They did not have time for taunts or unreasonable neighbours or relatives. They knew that probably isolation, fear and lack of support is what will follow them wherever they go and whatever they do. They were on a mission to provide a better life for their son.

They understood that Dr Kamath was a common doctor for many of them. He treated each of his patients and their families with the same compassion and empathy that he had shown to Ashutosh. Once he changed his job, Rajesh purchased a new house. He moved to the outskirts of the city, where a group of like-minded families had built a village with all facilities—an alternative residential environment providing mental health and assisted living for families wherein there was at least one family member who suffered from autism. This was a township by itself, having its own school, hospitals, shopping malls, gardens, library, painting arena, therapy centres and also a research centre. They called it an *ashram*.

Every family staying there had a child who had been diagnosed as autistic. There were some families with elderly parents having a child as big as 40 years of age but were unable to do even the minor activities of their day. Rather than worrying about what happens to their adult child after them, they now were thankful for this wonderful *ashram* which was providing hope to them. Though their children could not fit into mainstream society, here they were cared for by volunteers, who would make sure that life would continue the same for the child in the future as well.

Rajesh and Shilpa were welcomed into this community. As they came to know about the common goals of everyone staying here, a sense of pride came up. Here, no one was ashamed of their children. It was because of some unknown genetic factor that their children were born in this manner. This did not give society the freedom to exploit them.

School here taught them more practical things where they could find a liking. They introduced books and studies along with their own resource materials and taught the students how to hold a pencil or crayon and how to use them in order to draw lines and slowly put them together to make letters. They had speech therapy for all the students, wherein doctors took special care of individual needs. The houses were custom-made so that students could try to do things by themselves even without the presence of their immediate caretakers. Ashutosh took a liking towards gardening. The butterflies in the garden seemed to soothe him. The little caterpillars and dragonflies seemed to talk to him. Putting his hands into the mud and looking at the baby plants sprouting up and growing to form buds, leaves, and flowers fascinated him.

His fear of the crowd seemed to vanish when he was with his neighbouring friends, his classmates in school, who perfectly accepted him just the way he was. Some were way too tall for him, but he did not mind. Shilpa was able to make out that he was sharing his space happily with friends who were 20 years and 30 years older than him too but had the heart and mind only of a 5-year-old.

Ashu wanted to be fast just like the butterflies. And in order to do so, he showed Amma that he wanted to follow the butterfly on skates. He started enjoying skating and could now move with the wind. He wanted to replicate the colours of the flowers and the butterflies, and he started doing so with the help of crayons and glitter pens. There was no noise now, no doorbells or no pokey neighbours. He could now freely talk to the creator too. No one needed to question whom he was speaking to now. It was a matter of time before Shilpa finally introduced him to letters and their combination of spinning words and a totally different world—a world of books!

Rajesh was comfortable with his new job, having provided him with the option of working from home along with the healthy growth of his son. Shilpa soon started volunteering at the hospital taking care of inmates as she would look after her own child. She could make out that Ashu would certainly grow to be an independent individual.

They travelled to the city at times, to meet his grandparents, who were proud of the decision taken by Rajesh and Shilpa. Dr Kamath was a visiting doctor at this hospital and knew all the students, the inmates and their families. He tried to bring them all together with a chain of brotherhood, each family caring for the other. As he handed out the prizes to all the 50 students, some of them in gardening, some in painting, some in crafts, some in colouring, he had a sense of fulfilment, satisfaction and achievement. And as he handed out the gold medal to Ashutosh for skating, he saw a very grateful Shilpa and a proud Rajesh looking at him with joy and gratitude in their eyes.

Ashutosh himself was now able to say slowly, 'Thank you, nice uncle.' His day was made! Shilpa remembered what Dr Kamath had told her when she met him for the first time. 'It's a play of letters. Let him learn at his own pace.' She was also learning along with these pure souls. Belief in the Almighty and Hope for the future was something that Shilpa would never give up on. It was this hope that she had held on to five years ago, and it was still this very hope that Shilpa was relying on for the coming years as well.

Ultimate Satisfaction

Shivali Singh

Half-full hourglass, droopy staring eyes,

I reason, my emptiness inside.

I try to fill back the lost grains,

But more is lost, as I go back in vain.

With a gentle touch from the light of dawn,

Hourglass lay balancing the pawns.

I smile and jerk off the tears!

Rinsing off, without any smear,

Place the hourglass upright,

With bold and calm delight,

Glance at the half-filled above,

Childlike excitement flows somehow.

Frozen memories good or bad,

I have lived the life I once had.

Slice of holding the relevant,

Life has been redeemed, benevolent.

Build myself with better insight,

Absorbing grace, avoiding plight.

I no longer feel disappointed,

As I'm done with all expectations.

I do have a dream for this life,

Climbing one step at a time.

Sculpting days, the profound way,

Fortified by sweet evocation.

My ultimate satisfaction,

Hope smiles, bright in continuation.

The Right One

Mallika Chandrasekhar

The right one,

Will come in,

The perfect way,

Seamlessly,

Into your life,

Into your heart,

Without doubt,

Or iota of fear.

The right one

Will fit right in.

The calm or chaos,

The history or past,

Of your life.

Won't even matter,

There will be an instant connection,

Effortless camaraderie.

The right one

Will enter as laughter,

That will feel like music,

And fill you with happiness,

Which will stay, like a song,

You'll start to believe in angels,

And fairies from the promised land,

Making everything else pale in comparison.

The right one,

Will right the wrong done

By others before,

Removing the need for expositions,

And tiring conversations.

The right one,

Will simplify life and,

Add significance to your existence.

The right one,

Won't arrive with a big bang,

Or an announcement,

Over a loudspeaker,

But instead like a soft breeze,

On a wearied heart.

The right one,

Will come like just another ordinary moment.

The Human Spirit

Mallika Chandrasekhar

It's an amazing,

A facet of human existence,

The human spirit,

Its resilience,

Its persistence,

Its artistry in,

Creating, inventing, innovating,

Reasons and avatars suitable,

To survive,

To conquer,

To overcome,

Ill-fate,

Tough luck,

Unfavourable destiny.

The human spirit,

Is indestructible,

Adamantine.

Through the darkness of the mind,

Through brokenness of the heart,

Through lovelessness and loneliness,

The human spirit finds a way,

To reach the light,

To hear the inner voice,

To heal the wounds,

Old and new.

The pneuma is incredible,

Its intelligence,

Its awareness,

Its wisdom,

Finding strength,

Overcoming weakness,

Choosing forgiveness over hate,

Seeking salvation instead of hurting.

The human spirit,

Is relentless,

In its constant pursuit,

Of happiness,

A higher self,

A state of bliss.

This human spirit never fails,

And the proof of this spirit,

Are you and me,

And all of us in the living world.

Choose Life

Deepika Chalke

My name is Tara; in the language of the ancients, it means a star, a thing that radiates light but sails in darkness.

Souls like me are brought into existence for a role and a purpose. I was created millions of years ago; to guide souls that wander into the mystical and dead-end realm between two universes back to their home universe. The space between universes is where souls come to disappear from the multiverse once and for all. Not all souls can find this space; only those that have lost the will to live in every universe will find this place.

My mission is to follow my heart. It's drawn to souls that must not annihilate; for some unknown, mysterious reason, the multiverse needs these souls, and my job is to ensure these souls don't perish in my realm. Whether the soul likes it or not, is willing or not, it must go back to the realm of the living if that's the will of the strange multiverse that we are a part of.

The thing to know about me is I have no family, but I hope someday I will meet my tribe. Though my soul's destined to serve the multiverse and the ancients, I long for a home, for a sense of belonging, or for eternal rest. I think blessed are those that have been given the love of a mother and the love of a father.

'She's here!' my heart whispered. This is my signal to stop a soul from embracing non-existence.

'Stop!' I say in a gentle whisper.

'Leave me alone.' The soul responds in an eerily calm voice. This almost always means—please don't leave me alone, I am petrified.

'I can't leave you alone,' I respond in a kind voice.

'You can't help me.' This almost always means—please help me.

I respond in a gentle voice—'I can't take away your pain and suffering. But I can understand why you want to do this.'

'Go to hell.' The soul responds in a dead voice. This almost always means—I am in hell; please tell me I am not alone.

'I am in hell every second,' I reply with a deep breath.

'Who are you?' The soul briefly looks away from the void towards me, curious and exhausted.

'I am in charge of shipping you back to your home.'

'I have no home.' The soul responds.

'Your home is your body and your destiny.'

'Really? Always felt like trauma and pain were my home.'

'You feel guilty, grief-stricken, abandoned, traumatised, that's why you are here. To free yourself from suffering.'

'I don't need a psychologist. I need freedom.'

'You are a loving, kind soul, so bright that souls across universes can feel your blinding light.'

'That doesn't make any sense.'

'You know you are loved by the multiverse, right?'

'No.'

'You are compassionate and caring, full of wonder and curiosity. You met cruel, brutal beings that brought upon you and your family—

a cruel, brutal destiny. Now you carry shame and pain, guilt and grief, believing you are not worthy of love and happiness. But you forget that all the cruelty, insanity, and monstrosities that came your way, did not dim your light, your love; all the monsters that made you suffer did not turn you into a monster.

That is why you must live. Your trauma didn't turn you into a villain. Your pain has cut you open, but you show up every day to do your dharma, walk your path, to do the right thing, take care of yourself and the ones you love, and to spread compassion and knowledge in the world. You are fighting tough battles by yourself, the fight few souls can win; the fight of doing what's right and wise when the world has wronged you and hurt you and pained you. That makes you a Star. And the multiverse loves Stars, so do I.'

The soul looked at me, eyes radiating pain and silent strength.

'I thought love saves you from pain and evil; it protects you and nurtures you; if your love and the love of the multiverse can't give me what I want and couldn't save me from a brutal destiny, what's the point of your love?' They are just empty words. The battered soul spoke in a calm voice.

'True love does not hinder a soul's path towards enlightenment, empowerment, and higher love; true love watches over you and stays with you in spirit as you grow and discover your gifts and fulfil your dharma. True love guides gently, it will help you fulfil your destiny and your soul's potential. True love will not take away the obstacles on your path; it will not prevent you from falling; it will not fight your battles for you; true love will not abuse your soul by making you surrender your power, turning you into a co-dependent, helpless, powerless soul.'

'So, it's my destiny to suffer and that's why I must continue to live?' The soul asked in a defeated voice.

'No. To suffer is not your destiny but it is part of the journey.'

'You are talking to a dead person. I died a long time ago when I lost the ones I love. I lost the life that I wanted, that I needed. I lost my soul.

I lost myself. I lost everything I loved. And nothing you do can give me what I have lost.'

'You are wrong about that. You can access the part of you that you lost. That part of you carries your will to live, your spark of life, your true self, your inner child.'

'And what would you want in return for helping me regain my spark of life?'

'Nothing. This is my purpose, my destiny.'

'How are you going to find me what I lost?' The restless soul asked in an angry voice.

'You are going to find what you lost, not me. Your true self has been waiting for you for a long, long time in this realm. But there's a price you must pay before you can unite with it.'

'Of course. What do you want?'

'You have to choose your true self, not the trauma. You lost your true self because you thought your trauma condemned you to a life of pain and suffering, you thought the gods wanted you to feel worthless and terrible, to forever be mired in hopelessness and grief, to sacrifice your life and live like a dead woman. I am here to tell you that this is not the will of the multiverse.

Trauma is part of the spacetime fabric of the multiverse, it is one chapter in the story of your life, what you do next is up to you. You are not helpless, not stranded, not empty, not weak. Stop playing dead because you are alive and needed. Will you allow yourself to be happy, to follow your dreams, and to believe in humanity and your world once again?'

'It can't be that simple. It isn't up to me.'

'It always was that simple. And it is up to you.'

'You mean I am allowed to be happy even if I lost what was most precious to me? Why should I live? What's the point? What should I replace what I lost with? There's this hole in my soul, where do I go to fill it? Why should I live when my family no longer lives? Why did I survive? BRING THEM BACK NOW. Please. I can't go on. It's wrong of me to live when they died in the accident.'

I can feel her pain, energy is no different than surrendering to utter hopelessness and despair.

'You must live because it's their wish. Their souls are no longer human; they chose to be Stars in a distant galaxy. And you are their daughter. You must carry their legacy, to be a Star, to radiate light while sailing in darkness.'

'You are lying.'

'I cannot lie. I have no reason to lie. They want me to pass this message onto you—you are a fighter and remember a fighter always wins.'

The soul howled in agony and crumpled to the floor. These were the words her parents often said to her since she was a little girl.

I sat next to her in silence, waiting to see if she needed a hug. She did not.

When her soul looked up, there was a sliver of light in her eyes, a glint of hope, a fire, an announcement.

'I am ready. I will go back to where I came from and I will fight to keep the light alive, and I will win this fight. Tell them I love them. Tell them I miss being daddy's little girl and the apple of my mother's eyes.' She smiled a beautiful, angelic smile. Her aura glowed a brilliant gold.

'They know you will win. They watch over you and so do I.'

We both took a deep breath.

'Thank you.' She whispered in a gentle voice.

'You are welcome.'

With that, the soul with the golden aura disappeared. I could read in her energy that she was going to turn her pain into strength by becoming a world-class boxer, bringing light to the dark, and inspiring girls to show up in the world from a place of strength no matter the trauma. As for me, every time I lead a soul back home, I feel happy, and it keeps me going. I suppose, for souls like me, my purpose and my soul are my home.

There Lies a Lie

Karan Bhanot

It is better to be alone in the world of lie,
As a glass of truth makes fibsters fly.

The conviction made one's departed pride,
To lie in the global village becomes a rite.

It's a better-known lie that is sole to hell,
But lying won't help as well.

You lied once, twice and thrice,
That is your sin and your vice.

A lie is a lie, life is a lie, and a lie cannot die,
Having said that, the truth is not easy as pie.

But on a concluding note,

The rope of lying is short,

The only need is to untie a knot.

You yourself are made out of lies,

Or you are, merely by definition, a living lie!

My Lady

Giridhar Uppala

You are just a lazy brat who is good for nothing,
These words stung like a sharp needle in my heart.
My then-girlfriend for two years told me this,
While she was cheating behind my back.

For two months and left me for the best,
I was so lost then with nowhere to go.
With my parents so busy with their business,
My heart is too weak to cope with the loss.

Every bruise was becoming a wound with days passing,
And every word took hard to get out with no strength left.
Was introduced to a daughter of dad's business colleague then,
We intended to marry each other.

I was so against it at the beginning,
But with all doors closed, I complied with them.
The ceremony was simple and quiet,
But my heart was filled with complex emotions.

Thought it was unfair to her,

While I am still not over my past girlfriend.

But I tied the knot nonetheless as per my parent's wishes,

Initially, it was so tough as we started living together.

I worked for my dad's company, and she used to write novels,

Is a popular author now, made me a proud husband.

Was so patient with me, and gave me time and space to open up,

And I did, I vent it out all to her one night,

With tears flowing from my eyes and my head in her lap.

She rubbed my hair with her fingertips gently

And sang a lullaby to put me to sleep.

That was the moment I was reborn again,

This time, not as the son of my parents, but as a husband of hers.

She became my ray of hope for life,

And I started breathing again, full of joy.

We started going to proper dates,

I fell in love with her quickly and my wounds started to heal.

There were no secrets between us,

She is the best thing that happened to me.

And she is the one thing that I want to cherish my whole life,

And with a smile, I bid farewell to you all.

As I know my lady will be waiting for me.

That's Hope in My Heart

Malika Mehta

I'm vacant, I think I'm in a void,

I'm genuinely devoid,

Devoid of love,

Devoid of care,

Devoid of peace,

I only wish my breaths could cease.

In the sunshine, in rain and in storm,

The only thing I wish to hear,

Are your whispers in my ears,

That makes me feel like you are so close.

In the moonlight in sky full of stars,

I wish I could remove my scars,

By rewriting our story.

Underneath my golden skin,

There are many secrets contained.

I still have all your bouquets and,

So far, the memories we have carved.

To me, you are still in my bone, blood and flesh,

But to you, I'm merely a mesh.

A mesh of tangled mess.

That needs care,

To be the empress.

Is that so you never caress?

That one day I might take away,

All that you have ever impressed.

I'm sure that you must've been depressed,

But that doesn't mean you could just leave me to walk on my own.

I close my eyes to see your happy face,

Hoping and begging for just your embrace.

Looking out through my window,

At the mountains far away,

I always think it's their beauty,

That could be felt right away.

And I hear the rain pouring heaven,

As if I'm holding your hands in Devon,

Shutting my mind and closing my eyes,

Imagining you in my arms,

Feeling your heartbeats,

Your hands touching my dry chapped lips,

This is the best I could feel in this void.

I'm feeling devoid,

Devoid of love,

Devoid of care,

Devoid of you,

I am devoid of you,

I see nothing but you,

I sense nothing but you.

Whenever I feel you,

We may have been apart,

But as my hope you will always be dwelling,

Dwelling on the walls of my heart

You will always be in my heart.

You will always be whole rather than a part!

A Glimmer of Hope

Sumakalyani Ganti

Cerebral palsy they said, and unresponsive limbs… as the adorable child lay astray,

Long days of despair and disdain, often ending in dismay,

It was time for a shimmering light, a gleaming shine… an awakening to arise and a battle to fight,

Looking within herself, in her pious mind for the strength to ignite.

With an endearing look at his innocent face,

Looking in anticipation for his slightest movement … outsiders as she braced,

Normal he seemed, to those motherly eyes of resilience,

Probably with chances of a recovery, with the magic of medical science.

Seldom a glistening eye, the past years in endurance,

An epitome of selfless service, without prejudice, but just patience,

With magic in their wands and sparkly dust to sprinkle,

Awaiting fairies was she, with mystical spells and glittering twinkle.

As they mentioned a cure, closing the distance,

Entwined and enthralled, she felt His essence,

Probably he would wake up, move around, smilingly call her mom,

With dreams in her eyes, hope in her heart, courage in her soul,
serene and calm.

In her eyes, it sparkled, shone brightly, with newfound vigour,

Glittering like a precious diamond, rare to decipher,

A ray of optimism, a glimmer of hope...never to fade,

A healing tomorrow, as she waited, with news cheerful to cascade.

MEET THE
AUTHORS

Kavita Singh

Kavita Singh is an entrepreneur by profession and a poet by heart. Writing is her passion. She believes, through writing, one can explore and see this beautiful life and universe from innumerable aspects. She has covered almost everything from Earth to space, history to the future, political to non-political, compliments to sarcasm, etc. in her writings. She writes in English, Hindi and German.

Anannya Tiwary

Anannya Tiwary is a 16-year-old poet who loves to pen down her thoughts. She has been writing for four years now and has won numerous poetry competitions, one of them being *Kavyanjali*—a poetry competition which was held by the Wildlife Institute of India. She fancies reading novels and plays the piano in her leisure time.

Carol Mitra

Carol is a poet born during the pandemic times and has written and published two of her own books, *A Sip of Poetry and 21 Grams.* She has been published in both the anthologies of *Poetry Soup* on an International platform and her books are available worldwide. She currently resides in New Delhi with her husband and two children and is a full-time poet and writer.

Gayatri Bhasker

Gayatri Bhasker is the editor of a children's e-magazine, *Kid's Galaxy*. She worked in the IT sector for 13 years after which she took a break from her career to spend time with her kids. This is her first heartfelt poem, written for her father. The writing felt cathartic when she was trying to deal with his profound loss. She continues to write in simple words that resonates with every person. She finds consolation in the thought that he is watching over her, as she keeps spotting a butterfly whenever she misses him!

Revathi Bhasker

Revathi Bhasker, an Economist, has been a banker, Campus Placements Co-ordinator, Personal Secretary to the Governor of a Rotary District and Project Manager of a prestigious Rs. 5 crore Government of India Project on Knowledge Economy. A cancer survivor, she believes in radiating happiness wherever she goes, conducting game shows, quizzes and the like. She is an avid gardener, a good cook and also indulges in story writing. She is keen to give back to society whenever and whatever she can.

RaShiMa Roy

RaShiMa Roy (Shalini Roy) is a writer and German language specialist. Her interests include films, books, music and travelling. She is also a Vipassana practitioner and has a keen interest in spirituality. She lives in Mumbai with her family.

Smruti Tilak

Smruti Tilak was born in Mumbai, the city of dreams. Obsessed with books since a younger age, Smruti began penning her own fiction only during the lockdown period. Her stories and poetries are simple and can be read and enjoyed by young minds, as she believes, today's generation has lost the connection with books. She enjoys cooking, and travelling and aspires to write a travelogue.

Anju Elizabeth Kurien

Anju Elizabeth Kurien is a great admirer of art who seeks self-expression through her drawings and words. The world of pencils, pens and blank papers is her asylum. Most of her writings accompany her drawings posted on social media platforms. She has penned several poems like *Healing, Unrequited, Numb* and many other pieces of

writing that lack proper titles. She aspires to create works of art to which her audience could easily connect yet with deeper layers of meaning.

Kirti Pradeep

Kirti is a German language trainer and has travelled and lived all over India, shifting locations and houses more than 35 times in 30 years due to her husband's defence postings. In the process, she acquired invaluable experiences in various cities and small towns, cultures and cuisines of our country and got to know people from all walks of life. Her inspiration for writing short stories comes from these experiences. She loves Mumbai and primarily lives here, regularly visiting her family and loved ones in Kerala and Chennai. Her profession also brings her in contact with a variety of people in India and Germany and yet another culture.

Mallika Chandrasekhar

Mallika Chandrasekhar is a psychotherapist and content writer by profession and a poet by passion. She has been writing for the last 35 years and still gets excited every time she sits to write something that inspires her. The trail of her thoughts and observations of life can be perused from her blogs and Instagram page. She is an avid book reader and a movie-goer which serves as fodder for her book and movie review blogs. She lives in Hyderabad and currently works as an Associate Creative Director at White Thoughts and Branding Advertising company. She has two teenage kids, one dog, and many dreams and personal aspirations that keep her very busy.

Dinaz Treger-Patel

Dinaz Treger-Patel is originally from Frankfurt with a rather interesting story behind her dual surname. A Counselling Psychologist by profession, she believes that if people choose, they have the ability to change their stories, and embodies this philosophy of hers at her core. An avid reader who feeds her curiosity by reading any genre that catches her attention. She enjoys dancing, dreams of riding a bike and is an animal lover. She enjoys her newfound love for travelling. In her free time, you'd find her either watching series, movies and anime or gazing at the clouds, moon and stars.

Pushpa Bhatt

A 66-year-old passionate runner living an enriched life, Pushpa Bhatt is a clinical nutritionist. A fitness enthusiast, she has run innumerable half marathons, 12 Full Marathons, including two world majors and Ladakh Full Marathon and 13 Ultras including Khardungla 72 km. She has travelled to 23 countries and loves to travel solo. A former HR professional and an entrepreneur, music, movies, poetry writing and reading are her passions. She describes herself as a genuine and spontaneous person, focussed and result oriented.

Supraja Raghuram

Supraja Raghuram is an Indian-origin artist, singer and creative thinker exploring life beyond the world of Finance. Inspired by her friends and family, she aims to publish her own book in 2023.

Subhashree S (SS)

A voracious reader and a polyglot, Subhashree, 16, hails from Bengaluru, India. She is highly inquisitive, observant, and passionate about the social sciences, with an inclination to history. Being born in a Tamil family and raised in two major Indian cities, Subhashree brings a fresh and culturally-diverse perspective to the table through her poetry and short stories.

However, writing is just one of the feathers in her cap; she is a Black belt in Taekwondo, a women's rights activist, and a blogger. She hopes to start a business venture by herself someday while being a full-time writer.

Shivali Singh

An educator with a post-graduate degree in electronics and a bachelor's degree in education, Shivali Singh is a positive person, happily married to Shri Digvijay Singh. She's a loving mom who believes in keeping herself updated with time while still holding her ground. She has been part of four anthologies and writes on various social platforms. She had a flare for writing which has become a passion since the fateful Covid-19 period. She has won awards in various poetry and debate competitions. Poetry to her is inspiration, expression, dealing and healing.

Tanushree Keshan

Tanushree Keshan, an 18-year-old poet hails from the north-eastern state of Assam. She has had a flare for creative writing from an early age. Her hobby has found expressions in poems that centre around varied issues. She is an ardent lover of nature and knits words of experience and scrutiny together. Looking at the world through her lens of poetry she views the world in her own unique way and illustrates it through her works. She has the catchphrase, "Always be poetic even in an anthology of proses", which talks about the spirit of being unique in our avenues.

Srishti Sareen

Srishti Sareen is an avid reader born and brought up in Ludhiana. Writing is what makes her feel alive and relieved. She started writing when she was in the tenth standard, and since then she never got over the era of satisfaction. Currently, she is hell-bent on the fact that she can't live through *The Book Thief* for the first time ever again.

Dimple Makkhija

Dimple Makkhija is a Spanish and Maths teacher. Along with teaching, she loves writing poems and articles in her free time. This anthology contains her first published work, which is excited to share with all the readers. She hopes that you enjoy reading her work as much as she enjoyed penning it down. Happy Reading!

Sumakalyani Ganti

Sumakalyani Ganti has a degree in Engineering. She loves writing and believes that it is healing in many ways. Having worked with children as a Value Education Teacher, she loves to mingle with kids, and interact and counsel them. She aspires to bring a change in the ethical beliefs and values of children at the grass-root level.

Her stories and poems are in very simple, lucid language. Her father has always been her source of inspiration and her husband has stood by her through all her endeavours. She resides in Hyderabad, India and is the mother of two wonderful children.

Deepika Chalke

Deepika enjoys running, travelling, hiking and being in Nature. She believes writing is a powerful way to connect with other humans and spread joy, healing, hope, wisdom and beauty into the world. She has self-published a poetry book called *The Stars and The Void* and has written travel articles for a magazine. She ran 105 half marathons in 365 days, surpassing the current Guinness world record for most half marathons in a year by a woman, which is 102. She was featured in local magazines for her running feat. She has a bachelor's degree in Engineering and a Master's in MIS.

Avinash Sadaphule

Avinash Sadaphule is a writer originally from Pune, India now settled in Australia. He has a Master's in Marketing from the University of Pune and an Engineering degree in Computers. After starting as an FMCG salesman, he embarked upon a career in the Software Industry. He likes to write from his personal experiences and

observations and some of his work has been published in newspapers and online media.

Apart from being a voracious reader, his interests include digital marketing, hiking, improving his Spanish language skills and cracking dad jokes. He has recently started broadcasting on the radio which he enjoys very much and hopes that his listeners do too.

Gairik Misra

Gairik Misra is a 22-year-old student of English Literature. Born in Jalpaiguri in West Bengal, he was always fascinated by Greek mythos and nature. He tries to find creative ways to express his feelings and emotions and it can be seen in his writings.

Karan Bhanot

Karan Bhanot describes himself as one who has a great sense of ideas and a splendid bucket of thoughts and who is creative, whimsical, euphonious and expressive. He has the ability to see into the heart of things and an ability to deal with important unconscious material. He is of the opinion that poetry not only makes you think but

makes you think about why this poem is tugging at your heartstrings.

Anushka Rathi

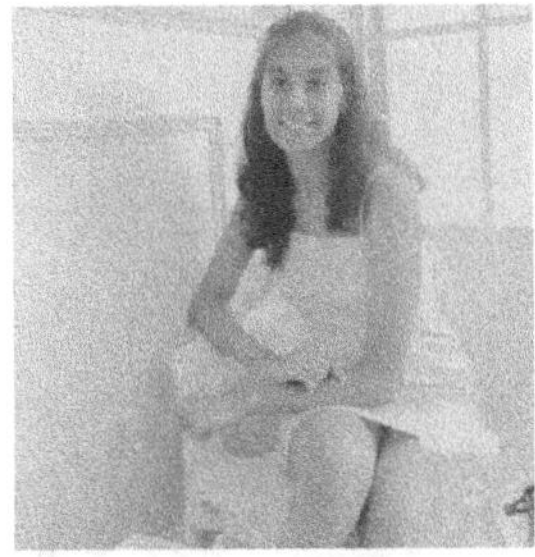

Anushka Rathi is a 17-year-old student residing and pursuing her education in Navi Mumbai. A trained classical dancer, she's always been a performer on the stage. She finds writing poetries and dancing a medium of expressing herself. An enthusiastic, lively and creative person, she finds comfort in socialising and having meaningful and interesting conversations.

Adwaith Jayan

Adwaith Jayan was born in 2003, in Kerala and raised in Coimbatore. He is an Engineering student and while growing up, he was fascinated by Bob Dylan and The Beatles, and this interest led to some exposure to poetry. Later, his interest grew into a pursuit of warmth from writing. He was charmed by many verses on many occasions and has decided to make some humble attempts.

Malika Mehta

Malika is a passionate being and possesses traits of empathy and sensitivity of the soul. Even though she is a calm and composed being, when overwhelming emotions flow through her mind, she pens them down and finds solace in writing. She wants to share glimpses of her subconscious with people who can relate to them.

Giridhar Uppala

Giridhar Uppala (*Maetostja*) is an aspiring story writer and poet. He is pursuing his engineering from IIT Jodhpur. An avid reader and a great fan of the Harry Potter series and fanfiction, he is also into film and screenwriting.

Sanika Sajan

She is currently pursuing her Master's degree in English Literature. She hails from Idukki, Kerala. She considers poetry as a medium to express inner thoughts and views. This is her second poem to get published. She enjoys both reading and writing in her leisure time.

INKFEATHERS PUBLISHING

www.inkfeathers.com

We love creating beautiful books for you!

Come be a part of our ever-growing community of authors.
Grow, write, and publish with us!

Scan here to explore
books, authors and more

Connect with us on socials. We'd love to hear from you!

    Inkfeathers Publishing